At Issue

How Should the U.S. Proceed in Iraq?

Other Books in the At Issue Series:

At Issue

How Should the U.S. Proceed in Iraq?

Bill Dudley, Book Editor

GREENHAVEN PRESS
A part of Gale, Cengage Learning

GALE
CENGAGE Learning

Detroit • New York • San Francisco • New Haven, Conn • Waterville, Maine • London

Christine Nasso, *Publisher*
Elizabeth Des Chenes, *Managing Editor*

© 2008 Greenhaven Press, a part of Gale, Cengage Learning.

Gale and Greenhaven Press are registered trademarks used herein under license.

For more information, contact:
Greenhaven Press
27500 Drake Rd.
Farmington Hills, MI 48331-3535
Or you can visit our Internet site at gale.cengage.com

For product information and technology assistance, contact us at

Gale Customer Support, 1-800-877-4253
For permission to use material from this text or product, submit all requests online at www.cengage.com/permissions

Further permissions questions can be emailed to permissionrequest@cengage.com

Articles in Greenhaven Press anthologies are often edited for length to meet page requirements. In addition, original titles of these works are changed to clearly present the main thesis and to explicitly indicate the author's opinion. Every effort is made to ensure that Greenhaven Press accurately reflects the original intent of the authors. Every effort has been made to trace the owners of copyrighted material.

Cover photograph reproduced by permission of © Todd Davidson/Illustration Works/Corbis.

ISBN-13: 978-0-7377-4056-1 (hardcover)
ISBN-13: 978-0-7377-4057-8 (pbk.)

Library of Congress Control Number: 2008924776

Printed in the United States of America
1 2 3 4 5 6 7 12 11 10 09 08

Contents

Introduction

In November 2006 the Democratic Party won narrow majorities of both the House and the Senate, ending a dozen years of Republican control of Congress. While analysts pointed to several issues that contributed to the defeat of the Republicans, including immigration, political scandals, and the economy, many agreed that the single most important issue voters were concerned about was America's ongoing war in Iraq. The war began in March 2003, when President George W. Bush, using authority granted by Congress in October 2002, made the decision to use military action to depose Iraq's longtime dictator, Saddam Hussein. By November 2006, the conflict had lasted thirty-two months, had claimed the lives of almost twenty-eight hundred U.S. soldiers, and appeared to have no end in sight.

Part of the growing public dissatisfaction with the Iraq War stemmed from its controversial beginnings. The rationale Bush provided for his March 2003 decision was that Iraq posed a significant threat to the United States and other nations because it might be developing weapons of mass destruction. Bush argued that Saddam had a documented history of developing, hiding, and using such weapons and was refusing to cooperate with United Nations resolutions mandating that Iraq prove it had no such weapons. Once the United States entered and occupied Iraq, however, no weapons of mass destruction were found. This led some people to conclude that the invasion was not worth the costs—or worse, that President Bush had been purposely misleading the American public when he argued that Iraq posed an imminent threat to them.

Much public disillusionment with the war stemmed not only because of failure to find weapons of mass destruction in Iraq, but because the ongoing conflict seemed to bring little progress toward peace or victory. In 2003, U.S. forces were at first extremely successful at defeating Iraqi army regiments, sweeping through the country and ending Saddam's regime and forcing the dictator into hiding. The stirring images and stories of America's easy initial victory in the first weeks of the war, however, faded over the next months and years as U.S. troops found themselves in the position of an occupying force in a complex and divided society.

Amidst growing calls for the United States to withdraw its troops from a deteriorating situation in Iraq, Bush, campaigning in 2006 for Republican congressional seats, argued that withdrawal would imply a defeat in Iraq and in the general American war against terrorism. He asserted that America must "stay the course" and not abandon its goal of stabilizing Iraq and ensuring that its newly elected and installed government would survive and be a positive force for American interests in the Middle East. The 2006 election results seemed to signal that the American people wanted a different course, but left unsure just what that course should be.

Some longtime war opponents redoubled their calls for the United States to immediately withdraw from Iraq, arguing that its original mission of deposing Saddam Hussein had been accomplished and that U.S. troop presence was only making things worse. A somewhat different recommendation came in December 2006 from the Iraq Study Group, a congressionally established commission of retired government officials. The group argued that the situation in Iraq was untenable and that the United States should plan a gradual troop withdrawal, pass on responsibility of keeping order to local Iraqi army and police units, and engage in a broad diplomatic initiative with neighbors in the Middle East to help ensure peace in the region. Many people predicted that President Bush, confronted with the 2006 political setback, would embrace this bipartisan proposal. Bush instead defied predictions and announced in early 2007 a different change in strategy—

what became known as the "surge." Bush announced to the nation in January 2007 that he was ordering an additional 30,000 troops to Iraq, increasing the number of soldiers there to 160,000. He also argued that his newly appointed Iraq military commander, General David Petraeus, would embrace a counterinsurgency strategy that emphasized protecting and winning support of the local populace rather than killing the enemy. Bush said the surge would help create stability and breathing space for the government in Iraq, led by its prime minister, Nouri al-Maliki, to bring together its various political parties, militias, and ethnic factions and make important political reforms to create a unified government and help bind the nation together. "Reducing the violence in Baghdad," Bush told the nation in announcing his surge strategy, "will help make reconciliation possible."

More than a year after November 2006, roughly another thousand soldiers had been killed, and financial costs of the Iraq War had risen to $100 billion a year, but opinion on the success of the "surge" was mixed. Supporters of Bush point to statistics that indicate that violence in Iraq has significantly decreased. The number of Iraqis killed in sectarian violence each month dropped from 3,000 in 2006 to less than half that number in 2007. The number of attacks on U.S. troops and Iraqi forces and civilians fell from 5,000 a month in late 2006 to 2,000 a month in late 2007. Anbar province, once the center of insurgent activity, saw the number of attacks fall from 1,350 in October 2006 to less than 100 per month in late 2007. Vice President Dick Cheney in a December 2007 interview called the surge "a remarkable success story" and predicted that by 2009 U.S. efforts will successfully create "a self-governing Iraq that's capable for the most part of defending themselves, a democracy in the heart of the Middle East, a nation that will be a positive force in influencing the world around it in the future." But opponents of the Iraq War argue that this tactical success has not been accompanied by any significant political reforms or compromises within the Iraq government and that Iraq remains a strategic blunder for the United States. "Iraq is moving in the direction of a failed state . . . with competing centers of power run by warlords and militias," argues Joost Hilterman of the International Crisis Group.

What seems to be beyond dispute is that Bush has successfully resisted any efforts by Democrats in Congress to influence or dictate American direction in Iraq, despite their new majority status. He has vetoed or otherwise blocked several measures mandating or requiring troop withdrawals and has been able to secure ongoing funding for the war. Most observers now agree that while debate over how the United States should proceed in Iraq will continue as long as U.S. troops remain there, significant changes in policy will come only after the 2008 elections send a new commander in chief to the Oval Office.

1

The United States Should Increase Diplomacy and Decrease Combat Troops

James A. Baker III and Lee H. Hamilton

The Iraq Study Group (ISG) was a bipartisan panel of public officials established and funded by Congress in 2006 to provide a consensus analysis of the situation in Iraq and U.S. policy options. It was headed by James A. Baker III, a Republican and former secretary of state under President George H.W. Bush, and Lee H. Hamilton, former Democratic member of Congress and chair of the House Committee on Foreign Affairs. After nine months of meetings, interviews with government and military officials, and consultations with experts, the ISG released its report on December 6, 2006.

The United States must enhance its diplomatic and political efforts to stabilize what is a serious and deteriorating situation in Iraq. It should engage Iraq's neighbors, including Iran and Syria, to help build an international consensus for regional stability. America should also change the primary mission of U.S. troops in Iraq from combat operations to supporting the Iraqi army and should begin removing combat forces from Iraq.

The situation in Iraq is grave and deteriorating. There is no path that can guarantee success, but the prospects can be improved.

In this report, we make a number of recommendations for actions to be taken in Iraq, the United States, and the region.

James A. Baker III and Lee H. Hamilton, "Executive Summary," *The Iraq Study Group Report*, 2006. Reproduced by permission.

Our most important recommendations call for new and enhanced diplomatic and political efforts in Iraq and the region, and a change in the primary mission of U.S. forces in Iraq that will enable the United States to begin to move its combat forces out of Iraq responsibly. We believe that these two recommendations are equally important and reinforce one another. If they are effectively implemented, and if the Iraqi government moves forward with national reconciliation, Iraqis will have an opportunity for a better future, terrorism will be dealt a blow, stability will be enhanced in an important part of the world, and America's credibility, interests, and values will be protected.

The challenges in Iraq are complex. Violence is increasing in scope and lethality. It is fed by a Sunni Arab insurgency, Shiite militias and death squads, al Qaeda, and widespread criminality. Sectarian conflict is the principal challenge to stability. The Iraqi people have a democratically elected government, yet it is not adequately advancing national reconciliation, providing basic security, or delivering essential services. Pessimism is pervasive.

If the situation continues to deteriorate, the consequences could be severe. A slide toward chaos could trigger the collapse of Iraq's government and a humanitarian catastrophe. Neighboring countries could intervene. Sunni-Shia clashes could spread. Al Qaeda could win a propaganda victory and expand its base of operations. The global standing of the United States could be diminished. Americans could become more polarized.

During the past nine months we have considered a full range of approaches for moving forward. All have flaws. Our recommended course has shortcomings, but we firmly believe that it includes the best strategies and tactics to positively influence the outcome in Iraq and the region.

External Approach

The policies and actions of Iraq's neighbors greatly affect its stability and prosperity. No country in the region will benefit in the long term from a chaotic Iraq. Yet Iraq's neighbors are not doing enough to help Iraq achieve stability. Some are undercutting stability.

The United States should immediately launch a new diplomatic offensive to build an international consensus for stability in Iraq and the region. This diplomatic effort should include every country that has an interest in avoiding a chaotic Iraq, including all of Iraq's neighbors. Iraq's neighbors and key states in and outside the region should form a support group to reinforce security and national reconciliation within Iraq, neither of which Iraq can achieve on its own.

Given the ability of Iran and Syria to influence events within Iraq and their interest in avoiding chaos in Iraq, the United States should try to engage them constructively. In seeking to influence the behavior of both countries, the United States has disincentives and incentives available. Iran should stem the flow of arms and training to Iraq, respect Iraq's sovereignty and territorial integrity, and use its influence over Iraqi Shia groups to encourage national reconciliation. The issue of Iran's nuclear programs should continue to be dealt with by the five permanent members of the United Nations Security Council plus Germany. Syria should control its border with Iraq to stem the flow of funding, insurgents, and terrorists in and out of Iraq.

The United States cannot achieve its goals in the Middle East unless it deals directly with the Arab-Israeli conflict and regional instability. There must be a renewed and sustained commitment by the United States to a comprehensive Arab-Israeli peace on all fronts: Lebanon, Syria, and President [George W.] Bush's June 2002 commitment to a two-state solution for Israel and Palestine. This commitment must include direct talks with, by, and between Israel, Lebanon, Palestinians (those who accept Israel's right to exist), and Syria.

As the United States develops its approach toward Iraq and the Middle East, the United States should provide additional political, economic, and military support for Afghanistan, including resources that might become available as combat forces are moved out of Iraq.

Internal Approach

The most important questions about Iraq's future are now the responsibility of Iraqis. The United States must adjust its role in Iraq to encourage the Iraqi people to take control of their own destiny.

The Iraqi government should accelerate assuming responsibility for Iraqi security by increasing the number and quality of Iraqi Army brigades. While this process is under way, and to facilitate it, the United States should significantly increase the number of U.S. military personnel, including combat troops, embedded in and supporting Iraqi Army units. As these actions proceed, U.S. combat forces could begin to move out of Iraq.

The primary mission of U.S. forces in Iraq should evolve to one of supporting the Iraqi army, which would take over primary responsibility for combat operations. By the first quarter of 2008, subject to unexpected developments in the security situation on the ground, all combat brigades not necessary for force protection could be out of Iraq. At that time, U.S. combat forces in Iraq could be deployed only in units embedded with Iraqi forces, in rapid-reaction and special operations teams, and in training, equipping, advising, force protection, and search and rescue. Intelligence and support efforts would continue. A vital mission of those rapid reaction and special operations forces would be to undertake strikes against al Qaeda in Iraq.

It is clear that the Iraqi government will need assistance from the United States for some time to come, especially in carrying out security responsibilities. Yet the United States must make it clear to the Iraqi government that the United States could carry out its plans, including planned redeployments, even if the Iraqi government did not implement their planned changes. The United States must not make an open-ended commitment to keep large numbers of American troops deployed in Iraq.

If the Iraqi government does not make substantial Progress . . . on national reconciliation, security, and governance, the United States should reduce its . . . support.

As redeployment proceeds, military leaders should emphasize training and education of forces that have returned to the United States in order to restore the force to full combat capability. As equipment returns to the United States, Congress should appropriate sufficient funds to restore the equipment over the next five years.

The United States should work closely with Iraq's leaders to support the achievement of specific objectives—or milestones—on national reconciliation, security, and governance. Miracles cannot be expected, but the people of Iraq have the right to expect action and progress. The Iraqi government needs to show its own citizens—and the citizens of the United States and other countries—that it deserves continued support.

Prime Minister Nouri al-Maliki, in consultation with the United States, has put forward a set of milestones critical for Iraq. His list is a good start, but it must be expanded to include milestones that can strengthen the government and benefit the Iraqi people. President Bush and his national security team should remain in close and frequent contact with the Iraqi leadership to convey a clear message: there must be prompt action by the Iraqi government to make substantial progress toward the achievement of these milestones.

If the Iraqi government demonstrates political will and makes substantial progress toward the achievement of milestones on national reconciliation, security, and governance, the United States should make clear its willingness to continue training, assistance, and support for Iraq's security forces and to continue political, military, and economic support. If the Iraqi government does not make substantial progress toward the achievement of milestones on national reconciliation, security, and governance, the United States should reduce its political, military, or economic support for the Iraqi government. . . .

It is the unanimous view of the Iraq Study Group that these recommendations offer a new way forward for the United States in Iraq and the region. They are comprehensive and need to be implemented in a coordinated fashion. They should not be separated or carried out in isolation. The dynamics of the region are as important to Iraq as events within Iraq.

The challenges are daunting. There will be difficult days ahead. But by pursuing this new way forward, Iraq, the region, and the United States of America can emerge stronger.

2

U.S. Military Withdrawal Would Harm America and the Middle East

George W. Bush

George W. Bush is the forty-third president of the United States.

The Iraq War should be considered in the context of a broader war against terrorism dating to September 11, 2001. That war will be ultimately won by transforming Middle East nations from incubators of Islam-inspired extremism into peace-loving democracies that renounce terrorism. Historical analogies to this war on terror can be found in World War II, the Korean War, and the Vietnam War—specifically the way these conflicts helped transform Asia into a region of democracies. Withdrawing U.S. troops from Iraq would embolden America's enemies and deny the power of freedom to the Iraqis and other Middle Eastern peoples.

I stand before you as a wartime President. I wish I didn't have to say that, but an enemy that attacked us on September the 11th, 2001, declared war on the United States of America. And war is what we're engaged in. The struggle has been called a clash of civilizations. In truth, it's a struggle for civilization. We fight for a free way of life against a new barbarism—an ideology whose followers have killed thousands on American soil, and seek to kill again on even a greater scale.

George W. Bush, "President Bush Attends Veterans of Foreign Wars National Convention, Discusses War on Terror," in address to Veterans of Foreign Wars, August 22, 2007.

We fight for the possibility that decent men and women across the broader Middle East can realize their destiny—and raise up societies based on freedom and justice and personal dignity. And as long as I'm Commander-in-Chief we will fight to win. I'm confident that we will prevail. I'm confident we'll prevail because we have the greatest force for human liberation the world has ever known—the men and women of the United States Armed Forces. . . .

Now, I know some people doubt the universal appeal of liberty, or worry that the Middle East isn't ready for it. Others believe that America's presence is destabilizing, and that if the United States would just leave a place like Iraq those who kill our troops or target civilians would no longer threaten us. Today I'm going to address these arguments. I'm going to describe why helping the young democracies of the Middle East stand up to violent Islamic extremists is the only realistic path to a safer world for the American people. I'm going to try to provide some historical perspective to show there is a precedent for the hard and necessary work we're doing, and why I have such confidence in the fact we'll be successful. . . .

I want to open today's speech with a story that begins on a sunny morning, when thousands of Americans were murdered in a surprise attack—and our nation was propelled into a conflict that would take us to every corner of the globe.

The enemy who attacked us despises freedom, and harbors resentment at the slights he believes America and Western nations have inflicted on his people. He fights to establish his rule over an entire region. And over time, he turns to a strategy of suicide attacks destined to create so much carnage that the American people will tire of the violence and give up the fight.

If this story sounds familiar, it is—except for one thing. The enemy I have just described is not al Qaeda, and the attack is not 9/11, and the empire is not the radical caliphate envisioned by Osama bin Laden. Instead, what I've described is the war machine of Imperial Japan in the 1940s, its surprise attack on Pearl Harbor, and its attempt to impose its empire throughout East Asia.

Today, the names and places have changed, but the fundamental character of the struggle has not changed.

Ultimately, the United States prevailed in World War II, and we have fought two more land wars in Asia. And many in this hall were veterans of those campaigns. Yet even the most optimistic among you probably would not have foreseen that the Japanese would transform themselves into one of America's strongest and most steadfast allies, or that the South Koreans would recover from enemy invasion to raise up one of the world's most powerful economies, or that Asia would pull itself out of poverty and hopelessness as it embraced markets and freedom.

The lesson from Asia's development is that the heart's desire for liberty will not be denied. Once people even get a small taste of liberty, they're not going to rest until they're free. Today's dynamic and hopeful Asia—a region that brings us countless benefits—would not have been possible without America's presence and perseverance. . . .

There are many differences between the wars we fought in the Far East and the war on terror we're fighting today. But one important similarity is [that] at their core they're ideological struggles. The militarists of Japan and the communists in Korea and Vietnam were driven by a merciless vision for the proper ordering of humanity. They killed Americans because we stood in the way of their attempt to force their ideology on others. Today, the names and places have changed, but the fundamental character of the struggle has not changed. Like our enemies in the past, the terrorists who wage war in Iraq and Afghanistan and other places seek to spread a political vision of their own—a harsh plan for life that crushes freedom, tolerance, and dissent.

Like our enemies in the past, they kill Americans because we stand in their way of imposing this ideology across a vital region of the world. This enemy is dangerous; this enemy is determined; and this enemy will be defeated.

We're still in the early hours of the current ideological struggle, but we do know how the others ended—and that knowledge helps guide our efforts today. The ideals and interests that led America to help the Japanese turn defeat into democracy are the same that lead us to remain engaged in Afghanistan and Iraq. . . .

Doubters and Skeptics

Many times in the decades that followed World War II, American policy in Asia was dismissed as hopeless and naive. And when we listen to criticism of the difficult work our generation is undertaking in the Middle East today, we can hear the echoes of the same arguments made about the Far East years ago.

In the aftermath of Japan's surrender, many thought it naive to help the Japanese transform themselves into a democracy. Then as now, the critics argued that some people were simply not fit for freedom.

Some said Japanese culture was inherently incompatible with democracy. Joseph Grew, a former United States ambassador to Japan who served as Harry Truman's Under Secretary of State, told the President flatly that—and I quote—"democracy in Japan would never work." He wasn't alone in that belief. . . .

Others critics said that Americans were imposing their ideals on the Japanese. For example, Japan's Vice Prime Minister asserted that allowing Japanese women to vote would "retard the progress of Japanese politics." . . .

There are other critics, believe it or not, that argued that democracy could not succeed in Japan because the national religion—Shinto—was too fanatical and rooted in the Emperor. Senator Richard Russell denounced the Japanese faith, and said that if we did not put the Emperor on trial, "any steps we may take to create democracy are doomed to failure." The State Department's man in Tokyo put it bluntly: "The Emperor system must disappear if Japan is ever really to be democratic."

Those who said Shinto was incompatible with democracy were mistaken, and fortunately, Americans and Japanese leaders recognized it at the time, because instead of suppressing the Shinto faith, American authorities worked with the Japanese to institute religious freedom for all faiths. Instead of abolishing the imperial throne, Americans and Japanese worked together to find a place for the Emperor in the democratic political system.

And the result of all these steps was that every Japanese citizen gained freedom of religion, and the Emperor remained on his throne and Japanese democracy grew stronger because it embraced a cherished part of Japanese culture. And today, in defiance of the critics and the doubters and the skeptics, Japan retains its religions and cultural traditions, and stands as one of the world's great free societies. . . .

The Korean War

Critics also complained when America intervened to save South Korea from communist invasion. Then as now, the critics argued that the war was futile, that we should never have sent our troops in, or they argued that America's intervention was divisive here at home.

After the North Koreans crossed the 38th Parallel in 1950, President Harry Truman came to the defense of the South— and found himself attacked from all sides. From the left, [investigative journalist] I.F. Stone wrote a book suggesting that the South Koreans were the real aggressors and that we had entered the war on a false pretext. From the right, Republicans vacillated. . . .

They never could decide whether they wanted the United States to withdraw from the war in Korea, or expand the war to the Chinese mainland. Others complained that our troops weren't getting the support from the government. One Republican senator said, the effort was just "bluff and bluster." He rejected calls to come together in a time of war, on the grounds that "we will not allow the cloak of national unity to be wrapped around horrible blunders."

Many in the press agreed. One columnist in *The Washington Post* said, "The fact is that the conduct of the Korean War has been shot through with errors great and small." A colleague wrote that "Korea is an open wound. It's bleeding and there's no cure for it in sight." He said that the American people could not understand "why Americans are doing about 95 percent of the fighting in Korea."

Many of these criticisms were offered as reasons for abandoning our commitments in Korea. And while it's true the Korean War had its share of challenges, the United States never broke its word.

Today, we see the result of a sacrifice of people in this room in the stark contrast of life on the Korean Peninsula. Without Americans' intervention during the war and our willingness to stick with the South Koreans after the war, millions of South Koreans would now be living under a brutal and repressive regime. The Soviets and Chinese communists would have learned the lesson that aggression pays. The world would be facing a more dangerous situation. The world would be less peaceful.

Instead, South Korea is a strong, democratic ally of the United States of America. South Korean troops are serving side-by-side with American forces in Afghanistan and in Iraq. And America can count on the free people of South Korea to be lasting partners in the ideological struggle we're facing in the beginning of the 21st century. . . .

Vietnam

Finally, there's Vietnam. This is a complex and painful subject for many Americans. The tragedy of Vietnam is too large to be contained in one speech. So I'm going to limit myself to one argument that has particular significance today. Then as now, people argued [that] the real problem was America's presence and that if we would just withdraw, the killing would end.

The argument that America's presence in Indochina was dangerous had a long pedigree. In 1955, long before the United States had entered the war, Graham Greene wrote a novel called, "The Quiet American." It was set in Saigon, and the main character was a young government agent named Alden Pyle. He was a symbol of American purpose and patriotism—and dangerous naivete. Another character describes Alden this way: "I never knew a man who had better motives for all the trouble he caused."

After America entered the Vietnam War, the Graham Greene argument gathered some steam. As a matter of fact, many argued that if we pulled out there would be no consequences for the Vietnamese people.

In 1972, one antiwar senator put it this way: "What earthly difference does it make to nomadic tribes or uneducated subsistence farmers in Vietnam or Cambodia or Laos, whether they have a military dictator, a royal prince or a socialist commissar in some distant capital that they've never seen and may [have] never heard of?" A columnist for *The New York Times* wrote in a similar vein in 1975, just as Cambodia and Vietnam were falling to the communists: "It's difficult to imagine," he said, "how their lives could be anything but better with the Americans gone." . . .

The world would learn just how costly these misimpressions would be. In Cambodia, the Khmer Rouge began a murderous rule in which hundreds of thousands of Cambodians died by starvation and torture and execution. In Vietnam, former allies of the United States and government workers and intellectuals and businessmen were sent off to prison camps, where tens of thousands perished. Hundreds of thousands more fled the country on rickety boats, many of them going to their graves in the South China Sea.

Three decades later, there is a legitimate debate about how we got into the Vietnam War and how we left. There's no debate in my mind that the veterans from Vietnam deserve the high praise of the United States of America. Whatever your position is on that debate, one unmistakable legacy of Vietnam is that the price of America's withdrawal was paid by millions of innocent citizens whose agonies would add to our vocabulary new terms like "boat people," "re-education camps," and "killing fields."

What Today's Terrorists Say About Vietnam

There was another price to our withdrawal from Vietnam, and we can hear it in the words of the enemy we face in today's struggle—those who came to our soil and killed thousands of citizens on September the 11th, 2001. In an interview with a Pakistani newspaper after the 9/11 attacks, Osama bin Laden declared that "the American people had risen against their government's war in Vietnam. And they must do the same today."

If we were to abandon the Iraqi people, the terrorists would be emboldened, and use their victory to gain new recruits.

His number two man, Zawahiri, has also invoked Vietnam. In a letter to al Qaeda's chief of operations in Iraq, Zawahiri pointed to "the aftermath of the collapse of the American power in Vietnam and how they ran and left their agents."

Zawahiri later returned to this theme, declaring that the Americans "know better than others that there is no hope in victory. The Vietnam specter is closing every outlet." Here at home, some can argue our withdrawal from Vietnam carried no price to American credibility—but the terrorists see it differently.

We must remember the words of the enemy. We must listen to what they say. Bin Laden has declared that "the war [in Iraq] is for you or us to win. If we win it, it means your disgrace and defeat forever." Iraq is one of several fronts in the war on terror—but it's the central front—it's the central front for the enemy that attacked us and wants to attack us again. And it's the central front for the United States, and to withdraw without getting the job done would be devastating.

If we were to abandon the Iraqi people, the terrorists would be emboldened, and use their victory to gain new recruits. As we saw on September the 11th, a terrorist safe haven on the other side of the world can bring death and destruction to the streets of our own cities. Unlike in Vietnam, if we withdraw before the job is done, this enemy will follow us home. And that is why, for the security of the United States of America, we must defeat them overseas so we do not face them in the United States of America. . . .

In Iraq, our moral obligations and our strategic interests are one. So we pursue the extremists wherever we find them and we stand with the Iraqis at this difficult hour—because the shadow of terror will never be lifted from our world and the American people will never be safe until the people of the Middle East know the freedom that our Creator meant for all.

I recognize that history cannot predict the future with absolute certainty. I understand that. But history does remind us that there are lessons applicable to our time. And we can learn something from history. In Asia, we saw freedom triumph over violent ideologies after the sacrifice of tens of thousands of American lives—and that freedom has yielded peace for generations.

The American military graveyards across Europe attest to the terrible human cost in the fight against Nazism. They also attest to the triumph of a continent that today is whole, free, and at peace. The advance of freedom in these lands should give us confidence that the hard work we are doing in the Middle East can have the same results we've seen in Asia and elsewhere—if we show the same perseverance and the same sense of purpose.

In a world where the terrorists are willing to act on their twisted beliefs with sickening acts of barbarism, we must put faith in the timeless truths about human nature that have made us free.

Across the Middle East, millions of ordinary citizens are tired of war, they're tired of dictatorship and corruption, they're tired of despair. They want societies where they're treated with dignity and respect, where their children have the hope for a better life. They want nations where their faiths are honored and they can worship in freedom.

Seeing the Iraqis through as they build their democracy is critical to keeping the American people safe from the terrorists who want to attack us.

And that is why millions of Iraqis and Afghans turned out to the polls—millions turned out to the polls. And that's why their leaders have stepped forward at the risk of assassination. And that's why tens of thousands are joining the security forces of their nations. These men and women are taking great risks to build a free and peaceful Middle East—and for the sake of our own security, we must not abandon them. . . .

There is one group of people who understand the stakes, understand as well as any expert, anybody in America—those are the men and women in uniform. Through nearly six years of war, they have performed magnificently. Day after day, hour after hour, they keep the pressure on the enemy that would do our citizens harm. They've overthrown two of the most brutal tyrannies of the world, and liberated more than 50 million citizens.

Progress in Iraq

In Iraq, our troops are taking the fight to the extremists and radicals and murderers all throughout the country. Our troops have killed or captured an average of more than 1,500 al Qaeda terrorists and other extremists every month since January of [2007]. We're in the fight. Today [August 2007] our troops are carrying out a surge that is helping bring former Sunni insurgents into the fight against the extremists and radicals, into the fight against al Qaeda, into the fight against the enemy that would do us harm. They're clearing the terrorists out of population centers, they're giving families in liberated Iraqi cities a look at a decent and hopeful life.

Our troops are seeing this progress that is being made on the ground. And as they take the initiative from the enemy, they have a question: Will their elected leaders in Washington pull the rug out from under them just as they're gaining momentum and changing the dynamic on the ground in Iraq? [My] answer is clear: We'll support our troops, we'll support our commanders, and we will give them everything they need to succeed.

Despite the mistakes that have been made, despite the problems we have encountered, seeing the Iraqis through as they build their democracy is critical to keeping the American people safe from the terrorists who want to attack us. . . .

A free Iraq is not going to transform the Middle East overnight. But a free Iraq will be a massive defeat for al Qaeda, it will be an example that provides hope for millions throughout the Middle East, it will be a friend of the United States, and it's going to be an important ally in the ideological struggle of the 21st century.

Prevailing in this struggle is essential to our future as a nation. And the question now that comes before us is this: Will today's generation of Americans resist the allure of retreat, and will we do in the Middle East what the veterans in this room did in Asia?...

The greatest weapon in the arsenal of democracy is the desire for liberty written into the human heart by our Creator. So long as we remain true to our ideals, we will defeat the extremists in Iraq and Afghanistan. We will help those countries' peoples stand up [as] functioning democracies in the heart of the broader Middle East. And when that hard work is done and the critics of today recede from memory, the cause of freedom will be stronger, a vital region will be brighter, and the American people will be safer.

3

U.S. Military Withdrawal Would Not Devastate America or the Middle East

Justin Logan

Justin Logan is a foreign policy analyst for the Cato Institute, a libertarian think tank.

The war in Iraq is similar to the Vietnam War in at least one respect—the arguments being made by President George W. Bush against withdrawal are similar to the arguments made by President Lyndon B. Johnson against U.S. withdrawal from Vietnam. In both cases, it is necessary to challenge the underlying assumptions in the presidents' arguments that the costs of admitting defeat and withdrawing are unacceptable. Both presidents argued that withdrawal would send the wrong message about U.S. credibility and perseverance, but if done right U.S. withdrawal from Iraq could strengthen America's credibility in the war against al Qaeda. The argument that U.S. withdrawal from Iraq would doom prospects for democratic reform in the Middle East ignores several realities: pressure from America, including military action, cannot force democracy in the Islamic world, and democracy in the form of elections is of questionable help in seeking a solution to America's terrorism problem. In Vietnam, thousands of U.S. soldiers died between 1967 and 1975 even though as early as 1967 some intelligence analysts recognized that victory was impossible and America could end the war without greatly harming its national interests. A similar analysis should be made of the war in Iraq.

Justin Logan, "Expect Setback, Not Catastrophe," *Cato Institute*, March 22, 2007. Copyright © 2007. Reproduced by permission of the author.

The [George W.] Bush administration has shifted noticeably from defending the Iraq war to emphasizing the suspected downsides of withdrawal. President Bush continually asserts that the consequences of leaving Iraq would be "grievous and far-reaching," and result in a "nightmare scenario." The president has focused on two negative consequences: a loss of U.S. credibility, and the prospect that withdrawal would precipitate a reverse domino effect, propping up the authoritarian governments that Bush's Iraq policy was intended to undermine. These claims echo the arguments of Lyndon Johnson, who argued against cutting our losses in Vietnam.

The issue of credibility was so central to America's Vietnam policy that tens of thousands of Americans died in the pursuit not of victory, but of saving face. They died because American leaders believed then—as the Bush administration apparently believes now—that defeat would have uncontrollable consequences. But the wiser voices inside the Johnson administration were arguing as early as the mid-1960s that the costs of defeat were manageable.

A Secret Memo

On Sept. 11, 1967, the intelligence community issued a secret memo titled "Implications of an Unfavorable Outcome in Vietnam." In it, the authors considered the many dire predictions that had been made about the dangers if the United States were to withdraw from Vietnam. The memo concluded that the perils of accepting an unfavorable outcome would be "probably more limited and controllable than most previous argument has indicated."

Further, the memo argued, "it should not be beyond the capacity of our leadership and diplomacy to negotiate this passage."

When the memo was written, fewer than 20,000 Americans had died in Vietnam. By the time the [Richard] Nixon administration finished whispering about a "decent interval," Vietnam had claimed the lives of more than 58,000 Americans.

Protecting America's Credibility

The issue of credibility is once again at the center of the debate over ending a disastrous American military enterprise. The Bush administration argues that U.S. allies would broadly question America's commitments, concluding that when the going gets tough, America bails out.

This argument is partially true, as it was in Vietnam. Al-Qaeda will indeed attempt to link our withdrawal to a larger narrative that includes President [Ronald] Reagan's [1983] retreat from Lebanon after the Marine barracks bombing in Beirut and our [1994] departure from Somalia after the Black Hawk Down incident. But unless our national leadership allowed our failure in Iraq to call into question other commitments, this damage certainly could be mitigated.

In the end, we face the same question as we did in Vietnam: Can the United States end the war and emerge with its fundamental global position unchanged?

Any administration extricating U.S. troops from Iraq would have to send the message that the U.S. military would now refocus its full attention on al-Qaeda. As for other commitments, why would we allow anyone to conclude that our failure in Iraq had any bearing on them? In withdrawing, the U.S. should answer questions of credibility loudly and clearly. Further, demonstrating that we recognize the error of our ways would indicate a seriousness of purpose and a national magnanimity that has been lacking throughout the Bush years.

Promoting Middle Eastern Democracy

The other protest from war supporters is that withdrawal would sound a death knell for the prospect of liberal democratic reform in the Middle East—a reversed version of the domino theory. But that objection implies that liberal democracy could sweep across the Islamic world if U.S. forces are kept in Iraq. In every location elections have been held in the Muslim world since the Iraq war—whether Egypt, the Palestinian territories, or Bahrain—something close to the worst possible result has emerged.

Elections predating significant social change have done little to advance either America's interests or the cause of liberalism itself. Similarly, the naive assertion peddled by neoconservatives that liberal democratic change was a workable solution to America's terrorism problem has been a blight on U.S. grand strategy. Reform in the Islamic world cannot be precipitated—or even hastened in a meaningful way—by pressure from America.

A Cautionary Tale

All this said, withdrawing from Iraq will indeed represent a defeat for the United States. It should be taken as a cautionary tale about the perils of nation building and the inadvisability of foreign-policy adventurism in general. But in the end, we face the same question as we did in Vietnam: Can the United States end the war and emerge with its fundamental global position unchanged? The 1967 memo offered the almost heretical view that "it seems unlikely that in the end an unfavorable outcome in Vietnam would greatly alter the present pattern of [power] relationships."

Four years [after America invaded Iraq in 2003], we should at least consider whether the same is true of Iraq.

4

Continuing U.S. Occupation of Iraq Harms America and the Middle East

Juan Cole

Juan Cole is a professor of Middle Eastern and South Asian history at the University of Michigan and a frequent media commentator on Middle Eastern affairs.

The reasons President George W. Bush presents for keeping U.S. troops in Iraq—that their presence prevents Iraq from becoming a stronghold of al Qaeda and the launching point for a regional war—are meant to scare the American people rather than accurately describe the situation in Iraq. It is actually the continuing presence of U.S. troops in Iraq that enables the Shiites, Sunnis, and Kurds to postpone or avoid making political compromises with each other, thus making civil war more likely. The United States must withdraw its troops in conjunction with a negotiated settlement between the warring parties in Iraq.

Both houses of Congress have now backed a timeline for withdrawal of US combat troops from Iraq in 2008, which George W. Bush has vowed to veto. [Bush did veto the spending bill with timeline; Congress eventually passed a spending bill without any timeline requirement.] gives two major rationales for rejecting withdrawal. At times he has warned that Iraq could become an Al Qaeda stronghold, at others that "a contagion of violence could spill out across the country—and

Juan Cole, "How to Get Out of Iraq," *The Nation*, April 23, 2007. Reproduced by permission.

in time, the entire region could be drawn into the conflict." These are bogeymen with which Bush has attempted to frighten the public. Regarding the first, Turkey, Jordan and Iran are not going to put up with an Al Qaeda stronghold on their borders; nor would Shiite and Kurdish Iraqis. Most Sunni Iraqis are relatively secular, and there are only an estimated 1,000 foreign jihadis in Iraq, who would be forced to return home if the Americans left.

Bush's ineptitude *has* made a regional proxy war a real possibility, so the question is how to avoid it. One Saudi official admitted that if the United States withdrew and Iraq's Sunnis seemed in danger, Riyadh [Saudi Arabia] would likely intervene. Turkish Foreign Minister Abdullah Gul has threatened to invade if Iraq's Kurds declare independence. And Iran would surely try to rescue Iraqi Shiites if they seemed on the verge of being massacred.

Driving Sunni Arabs to Violence

But Bush is profoundly in error to think that continued US military occupation can forestall further warfare. Sunni Arabs perceive the Americans to have tortured them, destroyed several of their cities and to be keeping them under siege at the behest of the joint Shiite-Kurdish government of Prime Minister Nuri Kamal al-Maliki. American missteps have steadily driven more and more Sunnis to violence and the support of violence. The Pentagon's own polling shows that between 2003 and 2006 the percentage of Sunni Arabs who thought attacking US troops was legitimate grew from 14 to more than 70.

The US repression of Sunnis has allowed Shiites and Kurds to avoid compromise. The Sunnis in Parliament have demanded that the excesses of de-Baathification be reversed (thousands of Sunnis have been fired from jobs just because they belonged to the Baath Party [formerly in power under deposed ruler Saddam Hussein]). They have been rebuffed. Sunnis rejected the formation of a Shiite super-province in the south. Shiites nevertheless pushed it through Parliament. The Kurdish leadership has also dismissed Sunni objections to their plans to annex the oil-rich province of Kirkuk, which has a significant Arab population.

U.S. Withdrawal Can Prevent Civil War

The key to preventing an intensified civil war is US withdrawal from the equation so as to force the parties to an accommodation. Therefore, the United States should announce its intention to withdraw its military forces from Iraq, which will bring Sunnis to the negotiating table and put pressure on Kurds and Shiites to seek a compromise with them. But a simple US departure would not be enough; the civil war must be negotiated to a settlement, on the model of the conflicts in Northern Ireland and Lebanon.

Talks require a negotiating partner. The first step in Iraq must therefore be holding provincial elections. In the first and only such elections, held in January 2005, the Sunni Arab parties declined to participate. Provincial governments in Sunni-majority provinces are thus uniformly unrepresentative, and sometimes in the hands of fundamentalist Shiites, as in Diyala. A newly elected provincial Sunni Arab political class could stand in for the guerrilla groups in talks, just as Sinn Fein, the political wing of the Irish Republican Army, did in Northern Ireland.

The United States took a step in the right direction by attending the March [2007] Baghdad summit of Iraq's neighbors and speaking directly to Iran and Syria about Iraqi security. Now the United States and Britain should work with the United Nations or the Organization of the Islamic Conference (OIC) to call a six-plus-two meeting on the model of the generally successful December 2001 Bonn conference on Afghanistan. The Iraqi government, including the president and both vice presidents, would meet directly with the foreign ministers of Iran, Turkey, Syria, Jordan, Saudi Arabia and Kuwait to discuss the ways regional actors could help end the war as the United States and Britain prepare to depart. Unlike the Baghdad summit, this conference would have to issue a formal set of plans and commitments. Recent Saudi consultations with Iranian leaders should be extended.

Saudi Arabia's Role

The Saudi government should then be invited to reprise the role it played in brokering an end to the Lebanese civil war at Taif in 1989, at which communal leaders hammered out a new national compact, which involved political power-sharing and demobilization of most militias. At Taif II, the elected provincial governors of Iraq and leaders of the major parliamentary blocs should be brought together. Along with the US and British ambassadors to Baghdad and representatives of the UN and the OIC, observers from Iraq's six neighbors should also be there.

By ending its occupation, the United States would go a long way toward repairing its relations with the Arab and Muslim world.

Saudi Arabia's King Abdullah has credibility with Iraq's Sunnis, especially now that he has denounced the US occupation as illegitimate. They could trust his representations, which would include Saudi development aid in places like Anbar province. Since the Sunnis are the main drivers of violence in Iraq, it is they who must be mollified, bribed, cajoled and threatened into a settlement. The Shiites will have to demobilize the Mahdi Army [a militia controlled by Shia cleric Muqtada al-Sadr] and Badr Organization [a militia linked with the Islamic Revolution in Iraq (SCRI), a Shiite party linked with Iran] as well, and Iran will have to commit to working with the Maliki government to make that happen. A UN peacekeeping force, perhaps with the OIC (where Malaysia recently proffered troops), would be part of the solution.

On the basis of a settlement at Taif II, the US military should then negotiate with provincial authorities a phased withdrawal from the Sunni Arab provinces. The Sunnis will have to understand that this departure is a double-edged sword, since if they continued their guerrilla war, the United States could not protect them from Kurdish or Shiite reprisals. Any UN or OIC presence would be for peacekeeping and could not be depended on for active peace-enforcing. The rewards from neighbors promised at Taif II should be granted in a phased fashion and made dependent on good-faith follow-through by Iraqi leaders.

Potential Rewards of Diplomacy

From all this the Sunni Arabs would get an end to the US occupation—among their main demands—as well as an end to de-Baathification and political marginalization. They would have an important place in the new order and be guaranteed their fair share of the national wealth. Shiites and Kurds would get an end to a debilitating civil war, even if they have to give up some of their maximal demands. The neighbors would avoid a reprise of the destructive Iran-Iraq War of the 1980s, which killed perhaps a million people and deeply damaged regional economies. And by ending its occupation, the United States would go a long way toward repairing its relations with the Arab and Muslim world and thus eliminate one of Al Qaeda's chief recruiting tools. A withdrawal is risky, but on the evidence so far, for the US military to remain in Iraq is a sure recipe for disaster.

5

A Multinational Effort Is Needed to Secure American Troop Withdrawal

Henry Kissinger

Henry Kissinger is a prominent foreign policy commentator and analyst who served as national security adviser and secretary of state in the 1960s and 1970s under Presidents Richard Nixon and Gerald Ford.

The United States cannot win a military victory in Iraq, but an abrupt withdrawal of U.S. troops from Iraq will result in chaos and violence in the Middle East that the United States can do little to control. The United States should develop regional governments within Iraq and work to enlist other nations to share the burden of stabilizing and rebuilding Iraq. Changing the American political and military campaign in Iraq into a multinational effort is the best way to secure U.S. troop withdrawal.

Two realities define the range of a meaningful debate on Iraq policy: The war cannot be ended by military means alone. But neither is it possible to "end" the war by ceding the battlefield, for the radical jihadist challenge knows no frontiers.

Problems with Abrupt Withdrawal

An abrupt withdrawal from Iraq will not end the war; it will only redirect it. Within Iraq, the sectarian conflict could assume genocidal proportions; terrorist base areas could reemerge.

Henry Kissinger, "Putting Politics Aside to Save Iraq," *International Herald Tribune*, September 17, 2007. Reprinted with permission.

Under the impact of American abdication, Lebanon may slip into domination by Iran's ally, Hezbollah; a Syria-Israel war or an Israeli strike on Iranian nuclear facilities may become more likely as Israel attempts to break the radical encirclement; Turkey and Iran will probably squeeze Kurdish autonomy; and the Taliban in Afghanistan will gain new impetus.

That is what is meant by "precipitate" withdrawal—a withdrawal in which the United States loses the ability to shape events, either within Iraq, on the anti-jihadist battlefield or in the world at large.

The proper troop level in Iraq will not be discovered by political compromise at home. If reducing troop levels turns into the litmus test of American politics, each withdrawal will generate demands for additional ones until the political, military and psychological framework collapses.

An appropriate strategy for Iraq requires political direction. But the political dimension must be the ally of military strategy, not a resignation from it.

Symbolic withdrawals, urged by such wise elder statesmen as Senators John Warner, Republican of Virginia, and Richard Lugar, Republican of Indiana, might indeed assuage the immediate public concerns. They should be understood, however, as palliatives.

The argument that the mission of U.S. forces should be confined to defeating terrorism, protecting the frontiers, preventing the emergence of Taliban-like structures and staying out of the civil-war aspects is also tempting. In practice, it will be very difficult to distinguish among the various aspects of the conflict with any precision.

Some answer that the best political result is most likely to be achieved by total withdrawal. In the end, political leaders will be held responsible—often by their publics, surely by history—not only for what they hoped but for what they should have feared.

Nothing in Middle East history suggests that abdication confers influence. Those who urge this course of action need to put forward what they recommend if the dire consequences of an abrupt withdrawal foreseen by the majority of experts and diplomats occur.

The missing ingredient has not been a withdrawal schedule but a political and diplomatic design connected to a military strategy. The issue is not whether Arab or Muslim societies can ever become democratic; it is whether they can become so under American military guidance in a timeframe for which the U.S. political process will stand.

Difficulty of Political Reconciliation

In homogeneous societies, a minority can aspire to become a majority as a result of elections. That outcome is improbable in societies where historic grievances follow existing ethnic or sectarian lines.

The United States is now in Iraq ... to serve the American commitment to global order and not as a favor to the Baghdad government.

Iraq is multiethnic and multisectarian. The Sunni sect has dominated the majority Shia and subjugated the Kurdish minority for all of Iraq's history of less than a hundred years.

American exhortations for national reconciliation are based on constitutional principles drawn from the Western experience. But it is impossible to achieve this in a six-month period defined by the [2007] American troop surge in an artificially created state wracked by the legacy of a thousand years of ethnic and sectarian conflicts.

Experience should teach us that trying to manipulate a fragile political structure—particularly one resulting from American-sponsored elections—is likely to play into radical hands. Nor are the present frustrations with Baghdad's performance a sufficient excuse to impose a strategic disaster on ourselves.

However much Americans may disagree about the decision to intervene or about the policy afterward, the United States is now in Iraq in large part to serve the American commitment to global order and not as a favor to the Baghdad government.

It is possible that the present structure in Baghdad is incapable of national reconciliation because its elected constituents were elected on a sectarian basis. A wiser course would be to concentrate on the three principal regions and promote technocratic, efficient and humane administration in each. More efficient regional government leading to substantial decrease in the level of violence, to progress toward the rule of law and to functioning markets could then, over a period of time, give the Iraqi people an opportunity for national reconciliation—especially if no region was strong enough to impose its will on the others by force.

Failing that, the country may well drift into de facto partition under the label of autonomy, such as already exists in the Kurdish region. That very prospect might encourage the Baghdad political forces to move toward reconciliation.

Need for International Diplomacy

The second and ultimately decisive route to overcoming the Iraqi crisis is through international diplomacy. Today the United States is bearing the major burden for regional security militarily, politically and economically.

Yet many other nations know that their internal security and, in some cases, their survival will be affected by the outcome in Iraq and are bound to be concerned that they may all face unpredictable risks if the situation gets out of control.

That passivity cannot last. The best way for other countries to give effect to their concerns is to participate in the construction of a civil society. The best way for us to foster it is to turn reconstruction step-by-step into a cooperative international effort under multilateral management.

It will not be possible to achieve these objectives in a single, dramatic move. The military outcome in Iraq will ultimately have to be reflected in some international recognition and some international enforcement of its provisions. The international conference of Iraq's neighbors, including the permanent members of the Security Council, has established a possible forum for this. A UN [United Nations] role in fostering such a political outcome could be helpful.

Such a strategy is the best road to reduce America's military presence in the long run.

None of these objectives can be realized, however, unless two conditions are met: The United States needs to maintain a presence in the region on which its supporters can count and which its adversaries have to take seriously. And above all, the country must recognize that bipartisanship has become a necessity, not a tactic.

6

U.S. Strategy Must Focus on Victory in Iraq

Newt Gingrich

Newt Gingrich was a Republican member of Congress from 1979 to 1999 and Speaker of the House from 1995 to 1999.

The United States is facing a worldwide enemy consisting of radical Islamic and other extremist individuals, groups, and nations seeking to harm and destroy America's system of government. Because of this, America cannot withdraw from Iraq or rely on the Iraqi government to defeat America's enemies. The United States must refocus and redouble its efforts to achieve victory in Iraq. The government must rethink its overall strategy and expand both its military and nonmilitary assets.

The United States finds itself in a global struggle with the forces of Islamic fascism and their dictatorial allies. . . .

We are confronted again and again with a worldwide effort to undermine and defeat the system of law and order which has created more prosperity and more freedom for more people than any previous system.

Threats to America

The threats seem to come in four different forms:

First, from individuals who are often self-recruited and randomly inspired through the internet, television and charismatic social and religious friendships.

Newt Gingrich, "Testimony Before the Senate Committee on Foreign Relations: The Cost of Defeat in Iraq and the Cost of Victory in Iraq," in www.claremont.org/projects/pageID.2493/default.asp, January 23, 2007.

Second, from organized nonstate systems of terror of which Al Qaeda, Hezbollah and Hamas are the most famous. Additional groups have sprung up and provide continuity, training, and support for terrorism.

Third, from dictatorships in the Middle East, most notably Iran and Syria, who have been consistently singled out by the State Department (including in 2006) as the largest funders of state-supported terrorism in the world. These dictatorships are investing in more advanced conventional weapons and in chemical and nuclear weapons.

Fourth, from a strange assortment of anti-American dictatorships including North Korea, Venezuela and Cuba.

This coalition of the enemies of freedom has growing power around the world. Its leaders are increasingly bold in their explicit hostility to the United States. . . .

These threats might be ignored if it were not for the consistent efforts to acquire nuclear and biological weapons by these enemies of freedom. . . .

Iraq in the Wider Context

The United States is now in a decaying mess in Afghanistan and an obviously unacceptable mess in Iraq.

While this language may seem harsh to defenders of the current policy, it is sadly an accurate statement of where we are.

Efforts to think through and solve the problems of Afghanistan and Iraq have to be undertaken in a context of looking at a wider range of challenges to American leadership around the world and potentially to our very survival as a country. . . .

With these caveats I want to focus on the challenge of Iraq.

Two Hard Paths Forward

America is faced with two very hard paths forward in Iraq.

We can accept defeat and try to rebuild our position in the region while accommodating the painful possibility that these enemies of freedom in Iraq—evil men, vicious murderers, and sadistic inflictors of atrocities—will have defeated both the millions of Iraqis who voted for legal self government and the American people and their government.

Alternatively we can insist on defeating the enemies of America and the enemies of the Iraqi people and can develop the strategies and the implementation mechanisms necessary to force victory despite the incompetence of the Iraqi government, the unreliability of Iraqi leaders, and the interference of Syria and Iran on behalf of our enemies.

Both these paths are hard. Both involve great risk. Both have unknowable difficulties and will produce surprise events.

Both will be complicated.

Yet either is preferable to continuing to accept an ineffective American implementation system while relying on the hope that the Iraqi system can be made to work in the next six months [beginning in January 2007].

There are three fundamental weaknesses in the current strategy.

I agree with the President on the supreme importance of victory [in Iraq].

America's Vital Interests

First, the strategy relies on the Iraqis somehow magically improving their performance in a very short time period. Yet the argument for staying in Iraq is that it is a vital *American* interest. If we are seeking victory in Iraq because it is vital to America then we need a strategy which will win even if our Iraqi allies are inadequate. We did not rely on the Free French to defeat Nazi Germany. We did not rely on the South Koreans to stop North Korea and China during the Korean War. When it mattered to American vital interests we accepted all the help we could get but we made sure we had enough strength to win on our own if need be.

President [George W.] Bush has asserted that Iraq is a vital American interest. In January 2007 alone he has said the following things:

> But if we do not succeed in Iraq, we will leave behind a Middle East which will endanger America in the future.

> [F]ailure in one part of the world could lead to disaster here at home. It's important for our citizens to understand that as tempting as it might be, to understand the consequences of leaving before the job is done, radical Islamic extremists would grow in strength. They would be emboldened. It would make it easier to recruit for their cause. They would be in a position to do that which they have said they want to do, which is to topple moderate governments, to spread their radical vision across an important region of the world.

> If we were to leave before the job is done, if we were to fail in Iraq, Iran would be emboldened in its pursuit of nuclear weapons. Our enemies would have safe havens from which to launch attacks. People would look back at this moment in history and say, what happened to them in America? How come they couldn't see the threats to a future generation?

> The consequences of failure are clear: Radical Islamic extremists would grow in strength and gain new recruits. They would be in a better position to topple moderate governments, create chaos in the region, and use oil revenues to fund their ambitions. Iran would be emboldened in its pursuit of nuclear weapons. Our enemies would have a safe haven from which to plan and launch attacks on the American people. On September the 11th, 2001, we saw what a refuge for extremists on the other side of the world could bring to

the streets of our own cities. For the safety of our people, America must succeed in Iraq.

Iraq is a central component of defeating the extremists who want to establish safe haven in the Middle East, extremists who would use their safe haven from which to attack the United States, extremists and radicals who have stated that they want to topple moderate governments in order to be able to achieve assets necessary to effect their dream of spreading their totalitarian ideology as far and wide as possible. This is really the calling of our time, that is, to defeat these extremists and radicals, and Iraq is a component part, an important part of laying the foundation for peace.

The inherent contradiction in the administration strategy is simple. If Iraq matters as much as the President says it does (and here I agree with the President on the supreme importance of victory) then the United States must not design and rely on a strategy which relies on the Iraqis to win.

On the other hand if the war is so unimportant that the fate of Iraq can be allowed to rest with the efforts of a new, weak, untested and inexperienced government then why are we risking American lives?

Both propositions cannot be true.

I accept the President's analysis of the importance of winning in Iraq and therefore I am compelled to propose that his recently announced strategy is inadequate.

The Failure of Civilian Agencies

The second weakness is that the current strategy debate once again focuses too much on the military and too little on everything that has not been working. The one instrument that has been reasonably competent is the combat element of American military power. . . .

The great failures in the Iraq and Afghanistan campaigns have been in non-combat power. Intelligence, diplomacy, economic aid, information operations, support from the civilian elements of national power. These have been the great centers of failure in America's recent conflicts. They are a major reason we have done so badly in Iraq.

The gap between the President's recent proposals and the required rethinking and transforming of our non-combat instruments of power is simply breathtaking.

No military leader I have talked with believes military force is adequate to win in Iraq. Every one of them insists that the civilian instruments of power are more important than the combat elements. They all assert that they can hold the line for a while with force but that holding the line will ultimately fail if we are not using that time to achieve progress in non-military areas.

This failure of the non-combat bureaucracies cannot be solved in Iraq. The heart of the problem is in Washington and that brings us to the third weakness in the current strategy.

The third weakness in the current strategy is its inability to impose war time decision making and accountability in Washington.

The interagency process is hopelessly broken.

This is not a new phenomenon. I first wrote about it in 1984 in *Window of Opportunity* when I asserted:

> [W]e must decide what sort of executive-branch planning and implementation system are desirable.

> At a minimum, we will need closer relationships between the intelligence agencies, the diplomatic agencies, the economic agencies, the military agencies, the news media and the political structure. There has to be a synergism in which our assessment of what is happening relates to our policies as they are developed and implemented. Both analyses and implementation must be related to the new media and political system because all basic policies must have public support if they are to succeed.

> Finally, once the professionals have mastered their professions and have begun to work in systems that are effective

and coordinated, those professionals must teach both the news media and the elected politicians. No free society can for long accept the level of ignorance about war, history, and the nature of power which has become the norm for our news media and our elected politicians. An ignorant society is on its way to becoming an extinct society. . . .

By the summer of 2003 it was clear the interagency was failing in Iraq and by September and October 2003 we were getting consistent reports from the field of the gap between the capability of the combat forces and the failure of the civilian systems.

No senior officer in the Defense Department doubts that the current interagency cannot work at the speed of modern war. They will not engage in a fight with the National Security Council or the State Department or the various civilian agencies which fail to do their job. But in private they will assert over and over again that the interagency system is hopelessly broken.

It was very disappointing to have the President focus so much on 21,500 more military personnel and so little on the reforms needed in all the other elements of the executive branch.

The proposals for winning in Iraq outlined below follow from this analysis.

Key Steps to Victory in Iraq

1. Place General [David] Petraeus in charge of the Iraq campaign and establish that the [American] Ambassador [in Iraq] is operating in support of the military commander.

2. Since General Petraeus will now have responsibility for victory in Iraq all elements of achieving victory are within his purview and he should report daily to the White House on anything significant which is not working or is needed.

3. Create a deputy chief of staff to the President and appoint a retired four star general or admiral to manage Iraq implementation for the Commander in Chief on a daily basis.

4. Establish that the second briefing (after the daily intelligence brief) the President will get every day is from his deputy chief of staff for Iraq implementation.

5. Establish a War Cabinet which will meet once a week to review metrics of implementation and resolve failures and enforce decisions. The President should chair the War Cabinet personally and his deputy chief of staff for Iraq implementation should prepare the agenda for the weekly review and meeting.

6. Establish three plans: one for achieving victory with the help of the Iraqi government, one for achieving victory with the passive acquiescence of the Iraqi government, one for achieving victory even if the current Iraqi government is unhappy. The third plan may involve very significant shifts in troops and resources away from Baghdad and a process of allowing the Iraqi central government to fend for itself if it refuses to cooperate.

7. Communicate clearly to Syria and Iran that the United States is determined to win in Iraq and that any further interference (such as the recent reports of sophisticated Iranian explosives being sent to Iraq to target Americans) will lead to direct and aggressive countermeasures.

8. Pour as many intelligence assets into the fight as needed to develop an overwhelming advantage in intelligence preparation of the battlefield.

9. Develop a commander's capacity to spend money on local activities sufficient to enable every local American commander to have substantial leverage in dealing with local communities.

10. Establish a jobs corps or civil conservation corps of sufficient scale to bring unemployment for [Iraqi] males under 30 below 10%. . . .

11. Expand dramatically the integration of American purchasing power in buying from Iraqi firms . . . to maximize the rate of recovery of the Iraqi economy.

12. Expand the American Army and Marine Corps as much as needed to sustain the fights in Iraq and Afghanistan while also being prepared for other contingencies and maintaining a sustainable rhythm for the families and the force.

13. Demand a war budget for recapitalization of the military to continue modernization while defeating our enemies. The current national security budget is lower as a percentage of the economy than at any time from Pearl Harbor through the end of the Cold War. . . .

14. The State Department is too small, too undercapitalized and too untrained for the demands of the 21st century. There should be a 50% increase in the State Department budget and a profound rethinking of the culture and systems of the State Department so it can be an operationally effective system.

15. The Agency for International Development is hopelessly unsuited to the new requirements of economic assistance and development and should be rethought from the ground up. . . .

16. The President should issue executive orders where possible to reform the implementation system so it works with the speed and effectiveness required by the 21st century.

17. Where legislation is needed the President should collaborate with Congress in honestly reviewing the systems that are failing and developing new metrics, new structures and new strategies.

18. Under our Constitution it is impossible to have this scale of rethinking and reform without deep support from the legislative branch. Without Republican Senator Arthur Vandenburg, Democratic President Harry Truman could never have developed the containment policies that saved freedom and ultimately defeated the Soviet Empire. The President should ask the bipartisan leaders of Congress to cooperate in establishing a joint Legislative-Executive working group on winning the war and should openly brief the legislative branch

on the problems which are weakening the American system abroad. Only by educating and informing the Congress can we achieve the level of mutual understanding and mutual commitment that this long hard task will require.

7

Immediate Withdrawal of All U.S. Troops Is the Best Strategy

Bill Richardson

Bill Richardson has served as a member of Congress, as the U.S. ambassador to the United Nations, and as Secretary of Energy. He took office as the governor of New Mexico in 2003.

America's continued military presence in Iraq is counterproductive, harmful to the American military forces, and serves no useful purpose. The only responsible choice for the United States is an immediate and total withdrawal of U.S. soldiers in Iraq. The American military is capable of planning and implementing such a withdrawal. Some soldiers can be redeployed to nearby nations such as Qatar and Bahrain to deal with al Qaeda and other threats.

Editor's note: The following viewpoint is taken from the author's speech to the Council on Foreign Relations during his bid for the 2008 Democratic presidential nomination.

It is an honor to be able to share ... my thoughts about how we can end the war in Iraq—and also to discuss some lessons which we must learn from this ongoing tragedy.

Over 3,800 brave Americans have lost their lives. Nearly 30,000 have been wounded—many very seriously; 170,000 are still at risk.

Bill Richardson, "Bill Richardson's Speech on Iraq Hard Choices: The Responsible Way Forward for Iraq and our Military,"*Council on Foreign Relations* (www.cfr.org), October 4, 2007. Reproduced by permission.

In addition to our troops, at least a hundred thousand Iraqi civilians have been killed in this conflict. Over four million more—fifteen percent of the country's population—have lost their homes and become displaced.

Ninety-three percent of Sunnis and over half the Shia think it's okay to shoot an American. The Iraqis want us out of their country.

Despite our best intentions, the American presence is not aiding the cause of peace—but rather contributing to the cycle of violence.

It did not have to be this way. Our military is the best-trained, best-equipped, most powerful fighting force in the history of the world. Tragically, the awesome power of our military has been matched in scale by the reckless incompetence of our civilian leadership. The President and Vice-President have blundered and mismanaged this conflict at every possible turn.

This catastrophe did not need to happen. Many of us, on the eve of this war, counseled greater diplomacy and more patience. Our warnings were ignored and the result has been the quagmire in which we find ourselves.

Whether we are Democrats, Independents or Republicans, all Americans want the violence to end. We all know that we must not allow the region to collapse into greater chaos and war. We all know how important it is that our military be strong and able to meet future threats. We all want our brave military men and women out of harm's way.

The question, going forward, is how we accomplish these goals.

Problems with Staying the Course

President [George W.] Bush says that we need to stay the course, indefinitely. He wants us to stick with a strategy that has failed week after week, month after month, year after year, in the hope that, finally—somehow—it will succeed.

Our troops have done all that they have been asked to do, with courage and professionalism, but no one can win someone else's civil war.

In the absence of political progress, our continued presence in Iraq is increasingly counter-productive. Our troops in Iraq are now the biggest obstacle to political change. If we stay on the present course, if we merely tinker with the mission as some have suggested, historians may look back on the first decade of this century as the moment in which the United States foolishly overstretched itself, beginning the long-term decline of American power and global leadership.

Only our departure can break the political stalemate and give us diplomatic leverage to promote reconciliation and regional diplomacy. The longer we stay, the more U.S. troops will die, the more Iraqi civilians will be killed, and the more elusive stability will become.

Delaying the inevitable is not a strategy. It is not useful. It is not responsible. It is not courageous. It is not moral.

I know that the President is wrong and you know he's wrong. He does not, and perhaps cannot, understand the dire reality of the situation. Throughout his Presidency, Bush has denied reality and avoided difficult choices. After 9/11, he sent the military to war, while he asked the nation to go shopping. In an all-out war against terror, he asked the country to be part-time patriots. We must stop this President and end this war.

The Only Responsible Choice

The foundation of my Iraq plan is this: *Get out now. Get all our troops out now.*

It is the only right and responsible choice.

Only when we are on our way out will Iraqis and others in the region start to see us as partners rather than as occupiers. Only then can a new political and diplomatic process begin. So long as we are there, with a bulls-eye on our back, the situation cannot change for the better.

Only by withdrawing *all* of our troops can we give our military the opportunity to rest, refit, and retrain.

Our military has been strained to the breaking point by this President. Our troops are serving longer tours in Iraq than they are spending with their families or training back at home—fifteen month tours. National Guard units are unable to perform essential missions here in the US where they are needed for homeland security. Much of our equipment is wearing down—and the corrosion of our hard power is limiting the leverage of our soft power.

Because of Iraq, we cannot focus on the real threats to our security. . . .

Because of Iraq, al Qaeda has been able to reconstitute itself. Today it is stronger than ever, training terrorists along the Pakistan-Afghanistan border.

Because of Iraq, we have lost the credibility we need to lead the world to stop nuclear proliferation and trafficking.

President Bush's failed strategy has made us both pariahs and patrons of both Sunni and Shia. We are both ally and enemy of Iraqi factions. And we subsidize their power struggles with American lives and dollars. This endless, multi-sided violence has muddied our strategic purpose. And the President's desperate refusal to face reality has confused our moral compass.

There is only one way to accomplish our objectives in Iraq. . . . Get ALL our troops out and get them out NOW.

I know this region. As US Ambassador to the United Nations, I spent eighty percent of my time on the Middle East. I have negotiated with many Arab and Muslim leaders, including the Saudis, the Iranians, even the Taliban. I stood toe-to-

toe with [former Iraqi leader] Saddam Hussein and got him to release American hostages. I understand the politics and the mentality of that part of the world.

Only once we make it clear that we are leaving can we expect the Iraqis to make the tough choices necessary for reconciliation. Only once all of our troops are on their way out, will others in the region do what they must to prevent Iraq from collapsing. Only our departure will give us the credibility to convene a Dayton-style reconciliation conference [like the one that established peace in Bosnia in 1995] to build a power-sharing arrangement policed by multilateral, UN-sanctioned peacekeepers.

To the extent that such a contingent is staffed by disciplined forces from non-neighboring Muslim countries, it will have a credibility which western troops simply don't have in that part of the world. And only when we leave can we expect rich countries from the region and elsewhere to help finance Iraq's reconstruction. . . .

There is only one way to accomplish our objectives in Iraq. There is only one responsible way forward: *Get ALL our troops out and get them out NOW.* . . .

Criticizing Democratic Rivals

After seven years of this Administration, we have come to expect that George Bush will make the wrong call on the important issues.

However, I expected more—much more—from my fellow Democrats in this race [for the 2008 Democratic presidential nomination].

Hillary Clinton, Barack Obama and John Edwards have said we have to wait and see how things go before we can know how many troops to bring out and how quickly. I say there has been enough waiting and seeing. If you haven't seen enough to know that we need to get all the troops out then you aren't watching the same war that I and the rest of

America are seeing. I don't think just changing the mission is enough—we need to end the war.

Senator Clinton has reportedly said that she might well have troops still in Iraq at the end of a second term—9 years from now. Senator Obama and John Edwards are unwilling to commit to removing all of the troops by the end of their first term—that's 5 years from now. I am opposed to 5 years or 9 years or any more years of our troops dying. My colleagues are wrong.

Military analysts have said that Senator Clinton's plan could require leaving up to 75,000 troops in Iraq.

That's changing the mission, not ending the war.

Obama and Edwards have said that they will pull our combat troops out, but they would leave thousands, tens of thousands of non-combat troops behind. Think of what this means: tens of thousands of support troops, unprotected, in the middle of a civil war.

That is changing the mission, not ending the war.

What do they think such a smaller force, with no combat protection, can accomplish that 170,000 troops could not?

I have asked them, over and over again, every chance I get. Their silence has been deafening.

I deeply respect my Democratic colleagues, but their plans simply will not end this war. It is going to take more than a sound bite and more than waiting and seeing—it is going to take decisive leadership.

Moving all the troops out quickly will require careful planning, but it can be done.

This is no time for political calculation or hopeful caution. Our troops' lives are on the line.

We need a responsible, comprehensive strategy to end the war and the strength to execute it.

We need to get all of our troops out. And we need to do it as quickly as possible.

What my colleagues are suggesting—a slow, protracted exit—will only multiply the casualties and delay political progress. President [Richard] Nixon chose such a slow departure from Vietnam. It led to 28,000 additional American deaths and perhaps another million Vietnamese deaths. And it accomplished nothing—soon after we left, the Communists took over.

A Fast Withdrawal Is Feasible

Moving all the troops out quickly will require careful planning, but it can be done. In accordance with Army doctrine, non-combat troops should leave the theatre first. Not the other way around as many of my colleagues suggest. Their approach would leave our men and women far more vulnerable.

We have rotated as many as 240,000 troops into and out of Iraq in a three-month period earlier in this war. After the first Gulf War, we redeployed a half million troops in a period of four months. As we redeploy, we also must work closely with Turkey to insure the stability of the border and the security of Kurdish areas.

Rapid maneuver is one of the time-honored strengths of our military. Swift movement saves lives—the longer a redeployment takes, the longer our brave troops will remain under fire. I have confidence in our armed forces. The naysayers who doubt our capability to get out rapidly and safely are wrong.

To rejoin the fight against the Taliban and Al Qaeda—and to encourage greater efforts by Pakistan and our NATO [North Atlantic Treaty Organization] allies, we should redeploy additional combat brigades to Afghanistan.

Some troops also must redeploy into quick strike forces based in the United Arab Emirates, Qatar, and Bahrain. Our military presence in friendly nations will enable us to meet new dangers and hit al Qaeda training camps wherever they might appear.

Respected experts like [former presidential adviser] Sandy Berger, [foreign policy scholar] Dr. Lawrence Korb, General William Odom, and General Robert Gard have looked at the evidence and come to similar conclusions to mine. . . .

Lessons for America's Military

The chaos and disorder in Iraq teach us that in today's world our armed forces need to defeat more than just armies. They also must defeat hatred and propaganda. Our military must be the fist that destroys our enemies—but it also must be a steadfast hand that creates a better peace.

We need to learn from Iraq and make sure that our military is prepared to deter, fight, and win the wars of the future. And to fight 21st century wars, we need a 21st century military.

One lesson we must learn is to give our Generals the numbers they need for post-war stabilization. Another lesson is to make sure that our troops are trained for the complex tasks they will face.

Ninety-seven percent of US deaths in the war have occurred after the end of so-called major combat operations. . . . We need to forge a military than can win both the war and the peace.

The military paradigm of this century will be what retired Marine Commandant General Charles Krulak (CREW-LACK) has called the three-block war. In this war, the lines between combat, stability, and humanitarian operations blur—soldiers deliver humanitarian aid on one block of a city, conduct stability operations on the next block, and fight an armed enemy on the third.

This is precisely what is happening in Iraq on a vast scale. Our military must be prepared for this new kind of war. Our military culture must adapt to this new reality. . . .

Hard Choices

The responsible way forward for Iraq and for our military will not be traveled easily. Hard choices lie ahead. We have to get out of Iraq, learn from errors made, and augment and reform our military so that it can meet the new challenges of a new era.

Difficult days indeed lie ahead, as we recover from the Iraq debacle, restore and modernize our military, and rebuild our reputation as a nation that leads others toward noble and worthy goals.

8

U.S. Troops Should Be Redeployed to Desert Bases in Iraq

Daniel Pipes

Daniel Pipes is a foreign policy analyst and director of Middle East Forum, publisher of the Middle East Quarterly.

Debate about U.S. policy in Iraq is polarized between those who advocate troop withdrawal and those who assert that U.S. troops should stay in Iraq and help rebuild that nation and create a successful democracy. The first option would be an unacceptable defeat for the United States, while the second option is not attainable given Iraqi resentment of foreign occupation. Fortunately, a third option exists: keep U.S. troops in Iraq, but redeploy them to remote desert bases in order to protect U.S. national interests, contain Iraq's neighbors, fight terrorist organizations, and assure free flows of oil and gas.

Two positions dominate and polarize the American body politic today [in 2007]. Some say the war is lost, so leave Iraq. Others say the war can be won, so keep the troops in place.

I split the difference and offer a third route. The occupation is lost but the war can be won. Keep U.S. troops in Iraq but remove them from the cities.

Predicting Failure for American Occupation

I already predicted failure for an American-led military occupation of Iraq in February 1991, right after the Kuwait War [in which The United States, under President George H.W. Bush, led an international coalition that drove Iraq out of Kuwait in 1991 but stopped short of occupying Iraq or deposing Iraqi leader Saddam Hussein] ended, writing then that an occupation lasting for more than some months "would probably lead to one of the great disasters in American foreign policy." I reached this conclusion on the basis of the Iraqi populace coming "very strongly to resent a predominantly American occupying force." Therefore, I concluded, as the ignominy of sniper fire buries the prestige of high-tech military superiority, "the famous victory achieved by Tomahawks, Tornadoes, and Patriots would quickly become a dim memory."

In April 1991, I added that "American troops would find themselves quickly hated, with Shi'is taking up suicide bombing, Kurds resuming their rebellion, and the Syrian and Iranian governments plotting new ways to sabotage American rule. Staying in place would become too painful, leaving too humiliating."

With the occupation a half-year old in October 2003, I forecast that "the mission in Iraq will end in failure" because the Iraqi motivation to remove coalition forces greatly exceeds coalition motivation to remain. "The US-led effort to fix Iraq is not important enough for Americans, Britons, or other non-Muslim partners to stick it out."

Troops should remain in Iraq [because] Iraq offers an unrivaled base from which to influence developments in the world's most volatile theater.

Now again, I reiterate that lack of will (how many Americans or Britons care deeply about Iraq's future course?) means that coalition forces cannot achieve the grandiose goal of rehabilitating Iraq. In calling for withdrawal, critics reflect the national mood that leaves the Bush administration increasingly isolated, a trend that almost surely will continue.

U.S. Troops Must Stay

But President George W. Bush is right to insist on keeping troops in Iraq.

In part, America's credibility is on the line. The country cannot afford what [author and military historian] Victor Davis Hanson notes would be its first-ever battlefield flight. The cut-and-run crowd deludes itself on this point. Senator George Voinovich (Republican of Ohio) holds that "If everyone knows we're leaving [Iraq], it will put the fear of God in them," to which Jeff Jacoby sardonically replies in the *Boston Globe*: sure, "Nothing scares al-Qaeda like seeing Americans in retreat."

The troops should remain in Iraq for another reason too: Iraq offers an unrivaled base from which to influence developments in the world's most volatile theater. Coalition governments can use them to:

- Contain or rollback the Iranian and Syrian governments.

- Assure the free flow of oil and gas.

- Fight Al-Qaeda and other international terrorist organizations.

- Provide a benign presence in Iraq.

At present, however, coalition forces barely have time to tend to these strategic goals, so bogged down are they with the tactical objectives they do least well—clearing alleyways, keeping the electricity flowing, protecting themselves from suicide bombers, defending the "Green Zone," and many other small-bore tasks.

I call for international troops to be released from improvised explosive devices, urban foxholes, and armed convoys, and redeployed to the deserts and borders where they and their high-tech equipment can play a strategic role.

Changing Our Goals

This implies the coalition abandoning its overly ambitious goal of a democratic, free, and prosperous Iraq, aiming instead for an Iraq that is secure, stable, and decent. In particular, holding elections in January 2005, a mere 22 months after the tyrant's [Saddam Hussein's] overthrow, was premature and unrealistic; Iraqis will need years, perhaps decades, to learn the subtle habits of an open society.

Removing Saddam Hussein was a realistic and welcome act of international sanitation but repairing Iraq in the face of a liberated, fractured, and ideological Iraqi populace remains beyond the coalition's will. The coalition gave Iraqis a fresh start; it cannot take responsibility for them nor rebuild their country.

Focusing on the strategic level also means the coalition distancing itself from Iraq's internal developments and treating Iraqis as adults shaping their own destiny, not as wards: no more hugging the country's leaders, treating its parliamentarians as subalterns, nor encouraging local partners to emigrate to Denmark or the United States.

That means staying the course but changing the course, redeploying to desert bases, not leaving Iraq.

9

Partial Withdrawals or Redeployments of U.S. Troops Will Not Work

Stephen Biddle

Stephen Biddle is a military and foreign policy expert at the Council on Foreign Relations and a former professor of national security studies at the U.S. Army War College.

Faced with growing public calls for U.S. troop withdrawal from Iraq, many observers have tried to craft compromise proposals that reduce troop levels in that nation but stop short of total withdrawal. But while compromise and moderation are often good instincts in foreign policy, in the case of Iraq such partial troop withdrawals are significantly flawed. They would leave the United States less able to control events on the ground within Iraq while making thousands of U.S. soldiers vulnerable targets. The United States should either greatly increase the number of soldiers in Iraq or withdraw completely.

Public support for the President's surge policy in Iraq [an increase in troops] is at a very low ebb. Yet many Americans remain reluctant to withdraw from Iraq altogether. The result has been growing interest in a variety of compromise proposals that would reduce US troop levels but stop short of total withdrawal. Are these sound choices for US policy?

The answer is no. Moderation and centrism are normally the right instincts in American politics. But Iraq is a very un-

Stephen Biddle, "Evaluating Options for Partial Withdrawals of US Forces from Iraq," *Council on Foreign Relations* (www.cfr.org), July 25, 2007. Reproduced by permission.

usual policy problem. For Iraq, centrist policies leave us with force postures that reduce our ability to control the environment militarily, but which nonetheless leave tens of thousands of US troops in the country to serve as targets. The result is likely to be the worst of both worlds: even less ability to stabilize Iraq than the surge offers, but with greater casualty exposure than a complete withdrawal would produce. Given this, the strongest case on the military merits lies at either of the two extremes in the current Iraq debate—a stronger analytical argument can be made for either surge or withdrawal than for the moderate proposals in between. . . .

The Case for the Surge

The surge represents a long shot gamble that is much likelier to fail than to succeed. But the odds of success, although small, are not zero. Given the consequences of failure in Iraq, even a long-shot chance at averting this is a defensible choice.

Iraq is already deep in civil warfare, and has been for at least two years. This civil war is currently being waged at relatively low intensity, and could easily escalate, but it is already a civil war all the same. The policy challenge in Iraq is thus civil war termination, not prevention. Unfortunately, efforts to negotiate peaceful settlements to civil wars rarely succeed prior to the military defeat of the weaker side. [Stanford political science professor] James Fearon, for example, who has performed perhaps the most rigorous empirical analysis of this problem, finds that of 54 civil wars since 1945, only about one-fourth ended in a peaceful negotiated settlement. And many of these efforts were not saddled with the legacy of prior misdiagnosis, policy error, and accumulated loss of public confidence that the United States now confronts in Iraq. Taken together, this legacy of error, combined with the inherent difficulty of the undertaking, suggest a poor prognosis for the American project in Iraq.

The odds in Iraq are thus long. But success is not inconceivable. . . .

Consequences of Failure

A long shot gamble is never an attractive option, but it can make sense if the costs of failure are high. And failure in Iraq could pose grave risks to American interests. If one defines failure as the total withdrawal of American forces from an unstable Iraq, then among the likely consequences of this are a major humanitarian disaster and a significant risk that the war could spread to engulf Iraq's neighbors.

The humanitarian consequences, for example, could be quite severe. US forces in Iraq are insufficient to end the violence, but they do cap its intensity. If we withdraw them, the violence will rise accordingly. Most victims of this violence are innocent civilians. The bitter ethnic and sectarian roots of this conflict give every reason to suspect that the scale of killing that could result from US withdrawal could dwarf today's death toll. . . .

An important advantage of complete withdrawal is to hasten the process of resetting our military to deal with the challenges of the post-Iraq security environment.

But the stakes go beyond the humanitarian. Each of Iraq's neighbors have vital interests in Iraq, and those interests create a serious risk that the war could spill over into a regional conflict spanning the entirety of the Middle East's primary energy producing states.

Should the worst case of a regional war emerge, the security and economic consequences for the US and our allies could be very grave: the spike one could expect in world oil prices should Mideast production be targeted in such a war could produce a major global economic contraction, imposing suffering on all, but especially on those living on the margins already, whether in the United States or abroad. And it is entirely possible that if confronted with such a disaster, the United States could be forced to re-intervene militarily in a conflict that will have gotten much harder still to resolve in the interim.

None of these prospects are certainties. But during the Cold War we worried enough about a very small risk of nuclear aggression by the Soviet Union to spend untold billions to reduce that small risk to an even smaller one. By comparison, the danger that we could catalyze an eventual regional war in the Mideast by failure in Iraq seems much more realistic. There is now no way to avert this risk with certainty, but the surge does offer at least a long shot chance to stabilize the country and thereby head off this prospect. As such it is a defensible, if unattractive, choice.

The Case for Complete Withdrawal

While a long shot chance at averting a possible disaster is defensible, so is the opposite. If the odds of success are now long, we are thus likely to fail anyway even if we try our best to avert this. And the cost of trying is painful: hundreds or thousands of American lives will be lost in the attempt that might otherwise be saved if we cut our losses and withdrew sooner. The likeliest outcome of the surge is eventual failure; this failure would lead to total US withdrawal anyway, but would postpone it until after many additional US fatalities were suffered. An earlier complete withdrawal of US forces ensures the failure but saves the added deaths.

The other chief advantage of complete withdrawal is an earlier recovery for the US military from the damage done by the war. The Army has estimated that it may take 2–3 years to replace or repair the equipment damaged by four years of continuous warfare in Iraq, even with the dedication of some $17 billion a year to the task. Every additional year of fighting not only postpones this rebuilding task, it lengthens it by adding to the backlog of unrepaired damage and deferred maintenance. Whatever the outcome in Iraq, we will need a capable military to respond to other potential threats elsewhere for decades to come. And if the surge does eventually fail we will confront the danger of a possible regional conflagration in the Mideast and its potential for US military involvement. These are serious policy challenges that continued high operating tempos in Iraq make it harder for us to meet. It may well be worth the cost in deferred rebuilding if an extended US effort succeeds and thus averts risks such as a regionalized war. But the likeliest case is that the surge will leave us with these risks and a significant delay in rebuilding the American military to meet them. Given this, an important advantage of complete withdrawal is to hasten the process of resetting our military to deal with the challenges of the post-Iraq security environment.

The [Bush] Administration has sometimes posed complete withdrawal as the only alternative to a surge, but used withdrawal as a strawman to encourage support for their policy. I agree with them that complete withdrawal is the best alternative to the surge, but I disagree with them on its merits: it *is* defensible, it is not a strawman.

This is not because it is risk-free or low cost. The dangers sketched above in the event of failure are real, and complete withdrawal sacrifices the chance to avert them via US-induced stability in Iraq. Moreover, the withdrawal itself is likely to be long, difficult, and dangerous. Even if we decide tomorrow to pull all US forces out of Iraq, it will take months to years simply to remove the many thousands of vehicles, weapons, pieces of equipment, and shipping containers of materiel that the United States has deployed to Iraq over the past four years. As we do so, we can expect to be attacked by Iraqi factions of all persuasions, whose incentives to prove themselves by demonstrating opposition to the defeated Americans will grow once we announce our departure. A United States departure from an unstable Iraq will probably be a fighting withdrawal.

But unless we succeed in stabilizing Iraq, those same difficulties and dangers await whether the withdrawal comes sooner or later. To fight our way out sooner means to avert the deaths we would suffer in a longer stay prior to the withdrawal; to delay is to add to the casualties of withdrawal the losses suffered beforehand. . . .

Reorienting Away from Combat

One of the most-discussed alternatives to either surge or complete withdrawal is partial withdrawal with the remaining troops reoriented away from combat missions and toward training and supporting the ISF [Iraqi Security Forces]. This is substantially less likely to succeed than the surge, however, and is likely to expose the US forces that remain to significant casualties all the same.

There are two chief problems here. First, since it is the US combat presence that now caps the violence level in Iraq's civil war, reducing that combat presence can be expected to cause the violence to increase accordingly. To be effective, embedded trainers and advisors must live with and operate with the Iraqi soldiers they mentor—they are not lecturers sequestered in some safe classroom. The greater the violence, the riskier their jobs and the heavier their losses.

> It is . . . unrealistic to expect that we can pull back to some safe but productive mission of training but not fighting.

Second, that same violence reduces their ability to succeed as trainers. There are many barriers to an effective Iraqi security force. But the toughest is sectarian factionalism. Iraq is in the midst of an ongoing communal civil war in which all Iraqis are increasingly forced to take sides for their own survival.

Iraq's security forces are necessarily drawn from the same populations that are being pulled apart into factions. No military can be hermetically sealed from its society—the more severe the sectarian violence, the deeper the divisions in Iraqi society become and the harder it gets for Americans to create the kind of disinterested nationalist security force that could stabilize Iraq. Under the best of conditions, it is unrealistic to expect a satisfactory Iraqi security force any time soon, and the more severe the violence, the worse the prospects.

The result is a vicious cycle. The more we shift out of combat missions and into training, the harder we make the trainers' job, and the more exposed they become. It is thus unrealistic to expect that we can pull back to some safe but productive mission of training but not fighting—this would be neither safe nor productive.

Reorientation to Border Security

Another proposal calls for withdrawing US forces from Iraq's cities, drawing down total US troop strength substantially, then deploying the remainder to Iraq's borders. These border defenses would perform some combination of two missions: preventing Iraq's neighbors from sending troops, weapons, or supplies into Iraq to reinforce sectarian factions; and discouraging Iraqi refugees from leaving the country and thus destabilizing neighboring states.

There are several problems with this option. First, Iraq's borders are not equally defensible. The western frontiers with Saudi Arabia, Syria, and Jordan are long but relatively easy to defend, as they are mostly open desert with a small number of isolated crossing points. The eastern frontier with Iran, however, is long and hard to defend, with much of it in difficult terrain and with a larger number of crossing points, many of which are more populated. With a limited US force stretched very thin to cover such an extended perimeter, it is very unlikely that the difficult eastern border could be defended adequately. The result would be a more porous eastern frontier, with a much greater throughput of weapons and assistance for Iranian efforts to aid their Shiite allies than for Saudi, Syrian, or Jordanian efforts to aid Sunni allies across the better-defended western frontier. Aside from the obvious disadvantage of enabling the Iranians to expand their influence at the expense of America's Sunni allies in Saudi Arabia and Jordan, this would also encourage Iraqi Sunnis to see the US as aligned with their Shiite enemies. After all, the net effect of the US mission would be to create a differential in the rate of external assistance that would systematically strengthen the Shiites relative to the Sunnis over time. And this would tend to drag us back into the conflict, as Sunnis increasingly seek ways to target the American presence whose effects are so disproportionately aiding their enemies. Whether this yields direct attacks on western border defenses (which would be easy for US forces to defeat in such open desert), or indirect attacks on US supply lines between its desert bases and its distant logistical hubs in Kuwait or elsewhere, the result would be an increasing prospect of combat for the reduced US posture left in Iraq.

Second, it is far from clear that US forces could legally prevent Iraqi refugees who wished to leave from doing so. We could encourage them to remain, perhaps by offering housing and relief aid in large, US-run refugee camps in the border area. But Iraqis who wished to leave would be difficult to detain without creating something that looked a great deal like the Soviet bloc's efforts to prevent Eastern European refugees from fleeing to the West during the Cold War. And if we did persuade large numbers to remain voluntarily in US-run desert refugee camps we would create for ourselves an enormous logistical and security challenge in itself. Historically, refugee camps frequently become bases and recruiting areas for guerillas and terrorists. The inevitable use of US-defended camps as havens for guerilla fighters in Iraq's civil war would draw the US back into the conflict unless we ran them like concentration camps (and possibly even if we did). Moreover the supply lines for isolated desert camps housing potentially thousands to millions of people would run through Iraqi cities in which the war would be raging and from which US troops had been withdrawn. Interdiction of these supply lines could lead to great suffering among large, disaffected refugee populations.

Third, the domestic politics of this option could be very difficult. This plan would leave tens of thousands of heavily armed US troops standing by a few miles away in the desert while Iraq's cities burned down in sectarian violence and thousands of innocent civilians died horrible deaths. The result would make for a very uncomfortable comparison with the Dutch standing by while Serbs slaughtered Muslim civilians at Srebrenica [in July 1995, during the civil war in Bosnia]; our ability to sustain such a posture in the midst of such imagery could be very problematic.

It is not clear that an American withdrawal . . . would cause [al Qaeda] to shift its focus from that immediate war in Iraq to terrorism against a distant America.

Reorientation to Counterterrorism

Several proposals call for a withdrawal from Iraqi cities, a reduction in US troops, and a reorientation of the remaining forces to a priority mission of fighting al Qaeda in Iraq (AQI) in order to reduce the danger of Iraq becoming a terrorist haven. Many have expressed concern that US failure in Iraq could enable al Qaeda to use the country as a base for planning terrorism against Americans; if we cannot stabilize the country at large, then perhaps we can at least prevent its use as a terrorist haven by continuing operations against AQI even as we withdraw the troops now engaged in other missions.

Here, too, there are several problems. First, our ability to fight AQI would diminish significantly if we withdrew our combat forces from Iraqi cities. The real challenge in counter-terrorism is finding the targets. And the chief means of doing this in Iraq is by persistent close contact with Iraqi civilians who have come to trust that US forces will remain to protect them against reprisals from AQI survivors if those civilians tip us off to AQI's locations. This kind of intelligence requires an extensive, long-term US troop presence in and among Iraqi civilians in the cities where they live. If we withdraw from those cities to remote bases in the desert, we thus lose our primary source of targeting information, leaving very few op-portunities for those troops to engage AQI.

Second, it is unclear how much of a terror risk AQI really poses, especially for targets in the United States. The relation-ship between Osama bin Laden's global organization and AQI, whose membership is largely Iraqi and whose focus is on Iraq itself, is complex. It is not clear that an American withdrawal that left behind an escalating civil war in Iraq would cause AQI to shift its focus from that immediate war in Iraq to ter-rorism against a distant America. Some have also speculated that al Qaeda outside Iraq would actually find its global cam-paign against the West undermined in the event of an all-out Sunni-Shiite civil war in Iraq, as its natural recruitment base in the Sunni Mideast turned from anger at the West toward anger at the more proximate Shiite enemy.

Moreover, AQI's ability to operate in Iraq rests on the will-ingness of Sunni Arabs to protect them with their silence, to provide safe houses and other support, and to tolerate their presence in their midst. If AQI lost this support, they would find it no easier to operate in Iraq than in any other state where they are an illegal organization without widespread support of the population. Yet AQI's support among Sunni Arabs is under challenge with the recent defection of the Sunni tribes that make up the Anbar Salvation Council. If these defections continue, AQI could find itself hard pressed even to sustain its position within Iraq, much less to establish an extensive base infrastructure for mounting attacks against a nation thousands of miles away.

Perhaps the Sunni tribal rebellion will spread to the point where Iraqi Sunnis will become so disaffected with AQI that they will provide us with intelligence even without a sustained US presence in their neighborhoods. If so, then such a withdrawal to the desert might not be as destructive of US intelligence prospects as one might normally suppose. But if so, then it is unclear why any significant ground forces would be needed in Iraq. If we can find the targets then we have plenty of ability to strike them even without significant ground forces nearby—air bases in Kuwait, Qatar, or elsewhere in the region would provide ample firepower for destroying terrorists whose location we can identify. The problem is identifying their locations. A plan to withdraw from Iraqi cities in order to fight AQI from desert bases is thus either impractical (if Iraqi Sunnis prove unwilling to provide intelligence without a promise of protection from nearby American troops) or unnecessary (if they offer intelligence even without the protection). Either way, it is far from clear that retaining substantial but reduced ground forces in Iraq and basing them in the open desert offers a meaningful capability to fight terrorism.

Finally, any plan to withdraw US troops from Iraq's cities and house them instead in desert bases is exposed to the same political disadvantages sketched above: it would leave heavily armed US soldiers standing on the sidelines nearby and watching passively as thousands of defenseless civilians are slaughtered in the cities we just left. To sustain such a posture in the face of the inevitable images on Western televisions could prove harder than we think.

Redeployment to Kurdistan

A final proposal would withdraw most US combat forces in Iraq but retain enough to defend our Kurdish allies. Kurdistan has been the most peaceful part of Iraq, and is the closest to functioning as a stable democracy. Even if we could not stabilize the rest of the country, perhaps it would make sense to retain enough military power in Iraq to defend this island of relative calm from the turmoil around it.

Here, too, however, there are important problems. As with other options that call for retaining US forces in Iraq but withdrawing them from Iraqi cities, a redeployment to quiet Kurdistan would pose major political challenges as those cities erupt in violence behind us.

Other difficulties are unique to the Kurdistan option. Among the more pressing of these concern US-Turkish relations, which have been deteriorating since prior to the 2003 invasion. A US withdrawal from the rest of Iraq to defend only Kurdistan would take a troubled relationship with Turkey and make it far worse. The Turks are deeply concerned with the threat of Kurdish separatism in southern Turkey. For years, Turkey has also been the target of Kurdish PKK [Kurdistan Workers' Party] terrorist attacks launched from Iraqi Kurdistan. While *we* might see a US withdrawal to defend only Kurdistan as a deterrent to Kurdish independence and PKK terrorism, *Turkey* is much more likely to see this as US defense for an independent Kurdistan against Turkish invasion; as a means of preventing Turkey from taking action to protect itself against the PKK; and as a major rallying point for Kurdish separatism in southern Turkey. The Turks already suspect that the United States hopes to replace them with an independent Kurdistan as the central American ally in the region; a US policy of abandoning Iraqi Arabs to their fate while establishing a US protectorate for Iraqi Kurds in the north would go a long way toward confirming this fear.

Some may argue that Turkish attitudes should take second place to defending a loyal US ally in Iraqi Kurdistan. Yet Turkey is a nation of 71 million, a NATO [North Atlantic Treaty Organization] ally, and a critical political, economic, and cultural bridge to Islam for the West. The damage to such an important relationship to be done by withdrawing US forces into Kurdistan must be weighed very carefully before turning to this as a means of justifying a middle-ground troop posture for Iraq.

The middle ground options of partial withdrawal are largely either self-defeating or unsustainable.

Perhaps most important, however, it is far from clear that such a redeployment could be sustained logistically without Turkish support. Kurdistan is more than 400 miles from the US logistical support base in Kuwait. If US combat forces withdraw from Iraq south of Kirkuk, supplies for forces in Kurdistan would have to be moved over literally hundreds of miles of undefended roads engulfed in bitter internecine civil warfare. This resupply effort would be extremely dangerous and very costly if it could be sustained at all. Without active Turkish support, the only alternative would be to supply the US garrison entirely from the air. But the cost of an open-ended commitment to support tens of thousands of combat troops for years through an airhead hundreds of miles from the nearest US logistical hub would be enormous—and especially so if that garrison came under attack from Iraqi factions reluctant to accept a US protectorate atop one of Iraq's most productive oil regions. Whether we value the US relationship with Turkey or not, the Turks could dramatically increase the cost of a US deployment in Kurdistan simply by refusing to permit us to resupply it across their border. Our ability to ignore their interests could thus have important limits.

Conclusions and Implications

None of these options are attractive or appealing. Four years of errors and missteps have left us in a position where our choices are now severely limited and none offer a high likelihood of success.

Yet some choices are nevertheless worse than others. In particular, the middle ground options of partial withdrawal are largely either self-defeating or unsustainable. If the remaining troops are reoriented to training, then the absence of US combat troops will undermine the training mission. If the remaining troops are reoriented to border defense, they will only be able to seal one side's border, creating a growing incentive for the other side to attack them. If the remaining troops are reoriented to counter-terrorism, the absence of US population security in Iraqi cities would deny us the intelligence we need to find targets for them. If the remaining troops are withdrawn to Kurdistan, the resulting damage to US-Turkish relations could undermine US interests in the region while possibly leaving us unable to support the garrison logistically.

On the whole, partial withdrawals thus tend to reduce our ability to control the environment militarily or stabilize Iraq— yet while leaving tens of thousands of US troops in the country to act as targets. The result is likely to be several more years of fruitless bloodletting in the midst of a deteriorating Iraq; if 160,000 troops cannot stabilize the country, our ability to do so with perhaps half that number must surely be far less. Partial withdrawal might—or might not—reduce the *rate* of American deaths in Iraq; there would be fewer Americans at risk, but if those who remain try to accomplish something then they could find their vulnerability greater in an environment that grows increasingly violent around them. Either way, however, partial withdrawal would not end American casualties. But it would make it even less likely that the lives we do lose would be lost for any purpose, or in exchange for any improvement in the future of Iraq. And any option that extends the US presence in Iraq also delays the rebuilding of the US military to meet other contingencies elsewhere. If this delay buys us a greater chance for stability in Iraq, then delay is defensible given the dangers of instability; but delays that do not buy us commensurate increases in the odds of success merely postpone US military reconstruction needlessly.

This is not to suggest that the extreme alternatives of surge or total withdrawal can offer a promise of low cost or strong odds for success, either. But the surge at least offers the greatest chances possible that the lives we lose would be lost for a reason. And total withdrawal at least limits the loss of American life to the greatest degree possible if we judge that the odds of success are simply too long. As such they offer advantages that partial withdrawals cannot.

10

The United States Should Support a Soft Partition of Iraq

Joseph Biden

Joseph Biden, a Democrat, has served as a U.S. senator from Delaware since 1972 and chairs the Senate Foreign Relations Committee.

America can withdraw most of its troops from Iraq without causing civil war or chaos by promoting the creation of three major provinces in which Kurds, Shiites, and Sunnis have significant control over their own regional governments. This plan, which is not true partition, would require the equal sharing of oil revenues, U.S.-provided reconstruction assistance, and a drawdown of U.S. troops. Such a division is the only realistic solution to the problem of sectarian and ethnic conflict within Iraq.

President [George W.] Bush does not have a strategy for victory in Iraq. His strategy is to prevent defeat and to hand the problem off to his successor. As a result, more and more Americans understandably want a rapid withdrawal, even at the risk of trading a dictator for chaos and a civil war that could become a regional war. Both are bad alternatives.

A Third Way

There is a third way that can achieve the two objectives most Americans share: to bring our troops home without leaving chaos behind. The idea is to maintain a unified Iraq by feder-

Joseph Biden, "Iraq: A Way Forward," in planforiraq.com, October 6, 2006.

alizing it and giving Kurds, Shiites and Sunnis breathing room in their own regions. The central government would be responsible for common interests, like border security and the distribution of oil revenues. The plan would bind the Sunnis—who have no oil—by guaranteeing them a proportionate share of oil revenues. It would convene an international conference to secure support for the power-sharing arrangement and produce a regional nonaggression pact, overseen by a Contact Group of major powers. It would call on the U.S. military to withdraw most U.S. troops from Iraq by the summer of 2008, with a residual force to keep Iraqis and their neighbors honest. It would increase economic aid but tie it to the protection of minority rights and the creation of a jobs program and seek funding from the oil-rich Gulf Arab states. The new, central reality in Iraq is deep and growing sectarian violence between the Shiites and Sunnis. In [the 2005] elections, 90 percent of the votes went to sectarian lists. Ethnic militias increasingly are the law in Iraq. They have infiltrated the official security forces. Massive unemployment is feeding the sectarian militia. Sectarian cleansing has forced at least 250,000 Iraqis to flee their homes in recent months. At the same time, Al Qaeda is now so firmly entrenched in Western Iraq that it has morphed into an indigenous jihadist threat. As a result, Iraq risks becoming what it was not before the war: a haven for radical fundamentalists.

The question I have for those who reject [soft partition] is simple: what is your alternative?

There is no purely military solution to the sectarian civil war. The only way to break the vicious cycle of violence—and to create the conditions for our armed forces to responsibly withdraw—is to give Shiites, Sunnis and Kurds incentives to pursue their interests peacefully. That requires an equitable and viable power-sharing arrangement. That's where my plan comes in. This plan is not partition—in fact, it may be the only way to prevent violent partition and preserve a unified Iraq. This plan is consistent with Iraq's constitution, which provides for Iraq's 18 provinces to join together in regions, with their own security forces, and control over most day-to-day issues. This plan is the only idea on the table for dealing with the militia, which are likely to retreat to their respective regions. This plan is consistent with a strong central government, with clearly defined responsibilities. Indeed, it provides an agenda for that government, whose mere existence will not end sectarian violence.

The example of Bosnia is illustrative. [In the mid-1990s], Bosnia was being torn apart by ethnic cleansing. The United States stepped in decisively with the [1995] Dayton Accords to keep the country whole by, paradoxically, dividing it into ethnic federations. We even allowed Muslims, Croats and Serbs to retain separate armies. With the help of U.S. troops and others, Bosnians have lived a decade in peace. Now, they are strengthening their central government, and disbanding their separate armies.

The course we're on leads to a terrible civil war and possibly a regional war. This plan is designed to head that off. I believe it is the best way to bring our troops home, protect our fundamental security interests, and preserve Iraq as a unified country.

The question I have for those who reject this plan is simple: what is your alternative?

A Five-Point Plan

1. Establish One Iraq, with Three Regions

- Federalize Iraq in accordance with its constitution by establishing three largely autonomous regions—Shiite, Sunni and Kurd—with a strong but limited central government in Baghdad

- Put the central government in charge of truly common interests: border defense, foreign policy, oil production and revenues

- Form regional governments—Kurd, Sunni and Shiite— responsible for administering their own regions

2. Share Oil Revenues

- Gain agreement for the federal solution from the Sunni Arabs by guaranteeing them 20 percent of all present and future oil revenues—an amount roughly proportional to their size—which would make their region economically viable

- Empower the central government to set national oil policy and distribute the revenues, which would attract needed foreign investment and reinforce each community's interest in keeping Iraq intact and protecting the oil infrastructure

3. Convene International Conference, Enforce Regional Non-Aggression Pact

- Convene with the U.N. [United Nations] a regional security conference where Iraq's neighbors, including Iran, pledge to support Iraq's power-sharing agreement and respect Iraq's borders

- Engage Iraq's neighbors directly to overcome their suspicions and focus their efforts on stabilizing Iraq, not undermining it

- Create a standing Contact Group, to include the major powers, that would engage Iraq's neighbors and enforce their commitments

4. Responsibly Drawdown US Troops

- Direct U.S. military commanders to develop a plan to withdraw and re-deploy almost all U.S. forces from Iraq by the summer of 2008

- Maintain in or near Iraq a small residual force—perhaps 20,000 troops—to strike any concentration of terrorists, help keep Iraq's neighbors honest and train its security forces

5. Increase Reconstruction Assistance and Create a Jobs Program

- Provide more reconstruction assistance, conditioned on the protection of minority and women's rights and the establishment of a jobs program to give Iraqi youth an alternative to the militia and criminal gangs

- Insist that other countries take the lead in funding reconstruction by making good on old commitments and providing new ones—especially the oil-rich Arab Gulf countries

What the Plan Is—and Is Not

Some commentators have either misunderstood the Plan, or mischaracterized it. Here is what the plan is—and what it is not:

1. *The Plan is not partition.* In fact, it may be the only way to prevent a violent partition—which has already started—and preserve a unified Iraq. We call for a strong central government, with clearly defined responsibilities for truly common interests like foreign policy and the distribution of oil revenues. Indeed, the Plan provides an agenda for that government, whose mere existence will not end sectarian violence.

2. *The Plan is not a foreign imposition.* To the contrary, it is consistent with Iraq's constitution, which already provides for Iraq's 18 provinces to join together in regions, with their own security forces, and control over most day-to-day issues. On October 11, [2006] Iraq's parliament approved legislation to implement the constitution's articles on federalism. Prior to

the British colonial period and Saddam's military dictatorship, what is now Iraq functioned as three largely autonomous regions.

But federalism alone is not enough. To ensure Sunni support, it is imperative that Iraqis also agree to an oil revenue–sharing formula that guarantees the Sunni region economic viability. The United States should strongly promote such an agreement. The final decisions will be up to Iraqis, but if we do not help them arrange the necessary compromises, nothing will get done. At key junctures in the past, we have used our influence to shape political outcomes in Iraq, notably by convincing the Shiites and Kurds to accept a provision allowing for the constitution to be amended following its adoption, which was necessary to secure Sunni participation in the referendum. Using our influence is not the same as imposing our will. With 140,000 Americans at risk, we have a right and an obligation to make known our views.

3. *The Plan is not an invitation to sectarian cleansing.* Tragically, that invitation has been sent, received and acted upon. Since the Samarra mosque bombing in February [2006], one quarter of a million Iraqis have fled their homes for fear of sectarian violence, at a rate [as of October 2006] approaching 10,000 people a week. That does not include hundreds of thousands of Iraqis—many from the professional class—who have left Iraq since the war. Only a political settlement, as proposed in the Plan, has a chance to stop this downward spiral.

4. *The Plan is the only idea on the table for dealing with the sectarian militia.* It offers a realistic albeit interim solution. Realistic, because none of the major groups will give up their militia voluntarily in the absence of trust and confidence and neither we nor the Iraqi government has the means to force them to do so. Once federalism is implemented, the militias are likely to retreat to their respective regions to protect their own and vie for power, instead of killing the members of

other groups. But it is only an interim solution, because no nation can sustain itself peacefully with private armies. Over time, if a political settlement endures, the militia would be incorporated into regional and national forces, as is happening in Bosnia.

5. *The Plan is an answer to the problem of mixed cities.* Large cities with mixed populations present a challenge under any plan now being considered. The essence of the Plan is that mixed populations can only live together peacefully if their leadership is truly satisfied with the overall arrangement. If so, that leadership will help keep the peace in the cities. At the same time, we would make Baghdad a federal city, and buttress the protection of minorities there and in the other mixed cities with an international peacekeeping force. Right now, the prospect for raising such a force is small. But following a political settlement, an international conference and the establishment of a Contact Group, others are more likely to participate, including countries like Saudi Arabia which have offered peacekeepers in the past.

6. *The Plan is in the self-interest of Iran.* Iran likes it exactly as it is in Iraq—with the United States bogged down and bleeding. But the prospect of a civil war in Iraq is not in Tehran's interest: it could easily spill over Iraq's borders and turn into a regional war with neighbors intervening on opposing sides and exacerbating the Sunni-Shiite divide at a time Shiite Iran is trying to exert leadership in the Islamic world. Iran also would receive large refugee flows as Iraqis flee the fighting. Iran, like all of Iraq's neighbors, has an interest in Iraq remaining unified and not splitting into independent states. Iran does not want to see an independent Kurdistan emerge and serve as an example for its own restive 5 million Kurds. That's why Iran—and all of Iraq's neighbors—can and should be engaged to support a political settlement in Iraq.

7. *The Plan is in the self-interest of Sunnis, Shiites and Kurds.* The Sunnis increasingly understand they will not re-

gain power in Iraq. Faced with the choice of being a permanent minority player in a central government dominated by Shiites or having the freedom to control their day-to-day lives in a Sunni region, they are likely to choose the latter *provided* they are guaranteed a fair share of oil revenues to make their region viable. The Shiites know they can dominate Iraq politically, but not defeat a Sunni insurgency, which can bleed Iraq for years. The Kurds may dream of independence, but fear the reaction of Turkey and Iran—their interest is to achieve as much autonomy as possible while keeping Iraq together. Why would Shiites and Kurds give up some oil revenues to the Sunnis? Because that is the price of peace and the only way to attract the massive foreign investment needed to maximize Iraqi oil production. The result will be to give Shiites and Kurds a smaller piece of a much larger oil pie and give all three groups an incentive to protect the oil infrastructure.

11

A U.S. Attack on Iran Can Salvage Victory in Iraq

Dan Friedman

Dan Friedman is a New York-based political commentator.

America's genuine victory over Saddam Hussein in 2003 has been marred by President George W. Bush's subsequent misman-agement of the American occupation of Iraq; however, Bush can salvage victory in Iraq by launching an air strike against Iran's nuclear facilities. Such an attack would not only destroy those facilities but would restore fear of and respect for America in that part of the world, give political advantage to the Republican Party, achieve momentum in America's war against terror, and enable the United States to withdraw from Iraq without losing face.

A recent story in the *New York Times* documented the steady proliferation of Halal food pushcarts in Midtown Manhattan, which I can attest to in my capacity as a sidewalk gourmet. These Muslim street food vendors—mostly Middle Eastern men who can be seen praying on mats beside their carts—are now nearly as ubiquitous, and popular, as New York's iconic hot dog stands. They deserve their success: the food is very good and it's priced right. Still, one might wonder whether this New York Jew [Friedman] living in a post-9/11 world finds the Big Apple's epicurean Islamicization a worri-some trend. No, honestly, I'm not nervous about it. Here's why.

Dan Friedman, "Where Bush Went Wrong in Iraq and How He Can Correct it Now," *American Thinker*, September 22, 2007. Reproduced by permission.

When I belly up for my chicken on pita, these men invariably greet me with cheerful deference, often referring to me as "boss." That polite gratuity is a clear sign they understand their standing in the melting pot can only be maintained through good citizenship and proper behavior. To put it bluntly, their instincts tell them the Muslim community isn't on top in polyglot America.

America's Moment of Triumph

Which brings us to the events of May 1, 2003. On that day President [George W.] Bush declared,

> Major combat operations in Iraq have ended. In the battle of Iraq, the United States and our allies have prevailed. And now our coalition is engaged in securing and reconstructing that country.

In short, it took 300,000 coalition troops just 42 days to overwhelm Saddam's army (then the only organized armed force in Iraq), send the brutal dictator into a dirt hole and take complete control of his country. According to the Department of Defense, on that date US military fatalities numbered 138 and our wounded totaled 542. [In late September 2007] those figures were 3,773 and 27,846, respectively.

For the sake of their sacrifices, we are obliged to recall the kind of country we inherited from Saddam Hussein on May 1, 2003. Listen to President Bush's description in a radio address five months earlier. Saddam, he said, is

> perhaps the world's most brutal dictator who has already committed genocide with chemical weapons, ordered the torture of children, and instituted the systematic rape of the wives and daughters of his political opponents. We cannot leave the future of peace and the security of America in the hands of this cruel and dangerous man.

Looked at another way, on the eve of our victory nothing moved in Saddam's Iraq and no Iraqi dared own so much as a

BB gun unless Saddam said it was OK. Thanks to Saddam's 24-year reign of terror, the country we seized was a pre-pacified nation. If its oppressed populace was not entirely happy to see us, they were physically and psychologically incapable of doing much about it. The remnants of its hostile leadership were on the run or in custody, the hated "Persians" were without any sway, "Iraqi insurgency" and "al Qaeda in Iraq" were two implausible oxymorons. An occupier's dream, putty in our hands, an Arab nation bloodied and bowed with the man in the street obliged to greet us with polite deference and ask, "hot sauce or white sauce, boss?" America was on top in Iraq—but it would not be for long.

It was precisely at his triumphant moment when George W. Bush lost Iraq, along with America's momentum in the war on terror, control of Congress in 2006, and the political assets needed to confront a radical Islamist Iran on the cusp of becoming a nuclear power—a threat that today makes Saddam's Iraq seem like a petulant child by comparison.

A Botched Occupation

Instead of putting first things first, namely, mounting an occupation modeled on our W[orld W[ar] II successes in Germany and Japan, then sealing Iraq's borders, declaring martial law, preparing for a long-term American regency, restricting movement within the country, and disarming the entire populace, Mr. Bush flew off-course. He parachuted in battalions of bureaucrats and constitutional lawyers, staking all on a rapid handover of power to his Iraqi designees and delivering "democracy" to an ancient people with no corresponding word in its language. In a part of the world where theology is the motive force, and the name of the only religion translates to "submit" in English, the president's jejune [weak] goodwill and misplaced egalitarianism signaled a willingness to replace a hard fist with an open hand. And that's when the bad guys in the Islamic world, conditioned by the laws of war found in their Quran, looked at each other in utter disbelief and shouted with glee, "last one to Iraq is a rotten egg!"

A well-executed allied occupation would have blunted the rise of today's lethal insurgency, kept al Qaeda, Iran and Syria on the sidelines, and cost far fewer Americans (and Iraqis) their lives. Also, ironically, it would have given Bush's political goals in Iraq a better chance to be realized than the remote possibility which exists for them now.

That's all 20-20 hindsight, sure, but it never hurts to know how we got from there to here—especially when it exposes a dangerously naïve institutional mindset that's still in place across the entire political spectrum. One that's balefully clueless about the nature of the Islamic enemy we're still battling within a struggle that's going to take many more difficult years to win. That's why it must be noted that virtually none of the "public intellectuals" on the right have owned up to the mistakes the administration has made in Iraq, and even fewer have owned up to their own benighted prognostications and Pollyannaish advice. There are exceptions—[conservative pundit] George Will is one.

> *All the blunders the President has committed to date in Iraq are reversible in . . . the time it will take to destroy Iran's fragile nuclear supply chain from the air.*

For the most part, though, the [journalist Charles] Krauthammers and the [journalist Norman] Podhoretzes of this world are content to blame the media, the frenzied Left and the Democratically-controlled Congress for the avoidable problems we are facing in Iraq. But those are the effects, not the causes, of the President's previous failures. At the outset, the media was gung-ho, begging to be "embedded" and ride shotgun with our troops, the Left is always in a frenzy, and it was his conduct of the war that cost Bush the Congress in '06.

How an Airstrike on Iran Will Help

Now for the good news. All the damaging consequences of all the blunders the President has committed to date in Iraq are reversible in 48- to 72-hours—the time it will take to destroy Iran's fragile nuclear supply chain from the air. And since the job gets done using mostly stand-off weapons and stealth bombers, not one American soldier, sailor or airman need suffer as much as a bruised foot.

Let's look downstream the day after and observe how the world has changed.

First and foremost, there's this prospective *fait accompli*—and it changes everything. The Iranians are no longer a nuclear threat, and won't be again for at least another decade, and even that assumes the strategic and diplomatic situation reverts to the *status quo ante* [the way it was before] and they'll just be able to pick up and rebuild as they would after an earthquake. Not possible.

Next, the Iranians would do nothing—*bupkes* [Yiddish: "nothing"]. They don't attack Israel, they don't choke off the world's oil supply, they do not send hit squads to the United States, there is no "war" in the conventional sense of attack-counterattack. Iran already has its hands full without inviting more trouble. Its leaders would be reeling from the initial US attack and they would know our forces are in position to strike again if Iran provokes us or our allies. They would stand before mankind with their pants around their ankles, dazed, bleeding, crying, reduced to bloviating from mosques in Teheran and pounding their fists on desks at the UN. The lifelines they throw to the Iraqi insurgents, Hezbollah [terrorist group] and Syria would begin to dry up, as would the lifelines the double-dealing Europeans have been throwing to Iran. Maybe the Mullahs [clerical leaders] would lose control.

Strong tremors would be felt throughout the Islamic *ummah* [community]. *"Just as we feared, they finally called our bluff. We pushed America to the limit and America pushed us* back twice as hard. *Look who's the dhimmi [non-Muslim living under Islamic law] now! Uh, maybe we need to rethink this 7th century Jihad crap—as well as the Jihadist idiots around here. This is all turning out to be more trouble than it's worth."*

Miracles would be seen here at home. Democratic politicians are dumbstruck, silent for a week. With one swing of his mighty bat, the President has hit a dramatic walk-off homerun. He goes from goat to national hero overnight. The elections in November [2008] are a formality. Republicans keep the White House and recapture both houses of Congress. Hillary [Clinton] is elected president—of the Chappaqua [New York] PTA.

Mr. Bush still has time to put America back on the offensive again.

Going forward, with Iran's influence blunted and the insurgents cut off, we end the war in Iraq on our terms. In his first hundred days, the new president reads Iraq the riot act and tells its leaders if they don't pull themselves together by a certain date, America will decide they're not worth the candle and we're going to get out.

Fighting the War on Terror

From that point on, with our arms free of the quicksand, we can fight the war on terror the way it should have been fought in the first place. Using our enormous edge in weapons, intelligence and technology, and building on it, we launch quick, lethal, ad hoc strikes wherever in the world we determine terrorists are working to harm us, shooting first and asking for permission later.

Am I dreaming? I don't think so. Being too sensible is probably more like it. In any event, I am not creating anything original here. . . . Mr. Bush still has time to put America back on the offensive again. But with only a little more than a year left in his term he has no time to lose. Rarely does history provide a failed wartime leader with such a golden opportunity for salvation.

Carpe diem [seize the day], Mr. President. The chicken pita is on me.

Organizations to Contact

The editors have compiled the following list of organizations concerned with the issues debated in this book. The descriptions are derived from materials provided by the organizations. All have publications or information available for interested readers. The list was compiled on the date of publication of the present volume; the information provided here may change. Be aware that many organizations take several weeks or longer to respond to inquiries, so allow as much time as possible.

American Enterprise Institute (AEI)
1150 Seventeenth St. NW, Washington, DC   20026
(202) 862-5800 • fax: (202) 862-7117
Web site: www.aei.org

The American Enterprise Institute for Public Policy Research is a scholarly institute that works to preserve limited government, private enterprise, and a strong foreign policy and defense. It has published several studies and articles arguing for a continued U.S. military presence in Iraq. AEI's Web site includes a Democracy in Iraq section that features writings on Iraq and on the war.

The Brookings Institution
1775 Massachusetts Ave. NW, Washington, DC   20036
(202) 797-6000 • fax: (202) 797-6004
e-mail brookinfo@brook.edu
Web site: www.brookings.org

The institution, founded in 1927, is a think tank that conducts research and education in foreign policy, economics, and government. Articles on Iraq can be found on the organization's Web site and in its publications, including the quarterly *Brookings Review*.

Center for American Progress (CAP)
1333 H St. NW, 10th Fl., Washington, DC   20005
(202) 682-1611
e-mail: progress@americanprogress.org
Web site: www.americanprogress.org

CAP is a progressively oriented think tank dedicated to improving the lives of Americans through ideas and action. Its publications include *Strategic Reset,* a detailed proposal for rethinking U.S. strategy in Iraq and the Middle East that includes the redeployment of U.S. troops from Iraq within one year.

Center for a New American Security (CNAS)
1301 Pennsylvania Ave. NW, Ste. 403
Washington, DC   20004
(202) 457-9400 • fax: (202) 457-9401
e-mail: info@cnas.org
Web site: www.cnas.org

CNAS is an independent and nonpartisan research institution that seeks to help inform and prepare strong, pragmatic, and principled national security and defense policies that promote and protect American interests and values. Its reports include "Phased Transition: A Responsible War Forward and Out of Iraq," which calls for reducing American troop presence in Iraq but leaving behind a smaller transitional force to fight terrorism and prevent regional war.

Center for Strategic and International Studies (CSIS)
1800 K St. NW, Washington, DC   20006
(202) 887-0200 • fax: (202) 775-3199
Web site: www.csis.org

The center works to provide world leaders with strategic insights and policy options on current and emerging global issues. It publishes books, including *Lessons of the Iraq War.* Articles, presentations, and other resources are available on its Web site.

Education for Peace in Iraq Center (EPIC)
1101 Pennsylvania Ave. SE, Washington, DC   20003
(202) 543-6176
e-mail: info@epic-usa.org
Web site: www.epic-usa.org

EPIC works to improve humanitarian conditions in Iraq and
to protect the human rights of Iraq's people. It opposed U.S.
military action in Iraq in 2003 and presently supports an increase in U.S. support for civil society, peace building, humanitarian relief, and responsible economic development in
Iraq. Information on its activities can be found on its Web
site.

Foundation for the Defense of Democracies
PO Box 33249, Washington, DC   20033
(202) 207-0190 • fax: (202) 207-0191
e-mail: info@defenddemocracy.org
Web site: www.defenddemocracy.org

A private nonprofit organization, the foundation works to
promote freedom and fight terrorism through research, jour-
nalism, and education. It supports a long-term U.S. military
commitment in Iraq as part of a broader struggle against Islamic terrorism. Articles and studies are available on its Web
site.

Middle East Forum
1500 Walnut St., Ste. 1050, Philadelphia, PA   19102
(215) 546-5406 • fax: (215) 546-5409
e-mail: info@meforum.org
Web site: www.meforum.org

The Middle East Forum is a think tank that works to define
and promote American interests in Iraq and other parts of the
Middle East. It publishes the *Middle East Quarterly*, a policy-
oriented journal. Its Web site includes articles on Iraq and
other topics as well as a discussion forum.

Middle East Media Research Institute (MEMRI)
PO Box 27837, Washington, DC   20038-7837
(202) 955-9070 • fax: (202) 955-9077
e-mail: memri@memri.org
Web site: www.memri.org

MEMRI translates and disseminates articles and commentaries from Middle East media sources and provides analysis on the political, social, and religious trends in the region. Its publications are available on its Web site.

Middle East Research and Information Project (MERIP)
1500 Massachusetts Ave. NW, Ste. 119
Washington, DC   20005
(202) 223-3677 • fax: (202) 223-3604
Web site: www.merip.org

MERIP is a nonprofit nongovernmental organization whose mission is to educate the public about the contemporary Middle East. It places particular emphasis on U.S. foreign policy, human rights, and social justice issues. It publishes the bimonthly *Middle East Report*.

Military Families Speak Out (MFSO)
PO Box 300549, Jamaica Plain, MA   02130
(617) 983-0710
e-mail: mfso@mfso.org
Web site: www.mfso.org

MFSO is an organization of citizens opposed to war in Iraq who have relatives or loved ones in the military. The group has contacts with military families in the United States and worldwide. The organization provides statements, articles, and links to other antiwar groups at its Web site.

Move America Forward
PO Box 1497, Sacramento, CA   95812
(916) 441-6197

e-mail: info@moveamericaforward.org
Web site: www.moveamericaforward.org

Move America Forward is a nonpartisan charitable organization committed to supporting America's troops and America's efforts to defeat terrorism. It opposes premature troop withdrawals from Iraq. Articles on its activities and special reports, including "A Brighter Future for Iraq," are available on its Web site.

U.S. Department of State
Bureau of Near Eastern Affairs, Washington, DC   20520
(202) 647-4000
Web site: www.state.gov/p/nea

The bureau deals with U.S. foreign policy and U.S. relations with Iraq and other Middle Eastern countries. Its Web site offers country information as well as news briefings and press statements on U.S. foreign policy.

Washington Institute for Near East Policy
1828 L St. NW, Ste. 1050, Washington, DC   20036
(202) 452-0650 • fax: (202) 223-5364
e-mail: info@washingtoninstitute.org
Web site: www.washingtoninstitute.org

The institute is an independent nonprofit research organization that provides information and analysis on the Middle East and U.S. policy in the region. It publishes numerous reports and studies, including "The Calm Before the Storm: The British Experience in Southern Iraq." Its Web site includes a special Focus on Iraq section that features articles and reports about that nation.

Bibliography

Books

Ali A. Allawi	*The Occupation of Iraq: Winning the War, Losing the Peace.* New Haven, CT: Yale University Press, 2007.
Liam Anderson and Gareth Stansfield	*The Future of Iraq: Dictatorship, Democracy, or Division?* New York: Palgrave Macmillan, 2004.
Rajiv Chandrasekaran	*Imperial Life in the Emerald City: Inside Iraq's Green Zone.* New York: Knopf, 2007.
Noam Chomsky	*Perilous Power: The Middle East and U.S. Foreign Policy.* Boulder, CO: Paradigm, 2007.
Wesley K. Clark	*Winning Modern Wars: Iraq, Terrorism, and the American Empire.* New York: PublicAffairs, 2003.
Anthony H. Cordesman	*Iraqi Security Forces: A Strategy for Success.* Westport, CT: Praeger, 2006.
Mike Evans	*The Final Move Beyond Iraq: The Final Solution While the World Sleeps.* Lake Mary, FL: Frontline, 2007.
James Fallows	*Blind into Baghdad: America's War in Iraq.* New York: Vintage, 2006.
Rick Fawn and Raymond Hinnebusch, eds.	*The Iraq War: Causes and Consequences.* Boulder, CO: Lynne Rienner, 2006.

Peter W.
Galbraith
The End of Iraq: How American Incompetence Created a War Without End. New York: Simon & Schuster, 2006.

Lloyd C. Gardner and Marilyn B. Young, eds.
Iraq and the Lessons of Vietnam, or, How Not to Learn from the Past. New York: New Press, 2007.

Leon T. Hadar
Sandstorm: Policy Failure in the Middle East. New York: Palgrave Macmillan, 2005.

Christopher Hughes
War on Two Fronts: An Infantry Commander's War in Iraq and the Pentagon. Havertown, PA: Casemate, 2007.

Iraq Study Group
The Iraq Study Group Report. New York: Vintage, 2006.

George S. McGovern and William R. Polk
Out of Iraq: A Practical Plan for Withdrawal Now. New York: Simon & Schuster Paperbacks, 2006.

George Packer
The Assassins' Gate: America in Iraq. New York: Farrar, Straus & Giroux, 2005.

Robert Patterson
War Crimes: The Left's Campaign to Destroy the Military and Lose the War on Terror. New York: Crown, 2007.

William R. Polk
Understanding Iraq. New York: HarperCollins, 2005.

Thomas E. Ricks
Fiasco: The American Military Adventure in Iraq. New York: Penguin, 2006.

Cindy Sheehan   *Peace Mom: A Mother's Journey Through Heartache to Activism.* New York: Atria, 2006.

Periodicals

Zbigniew Brzezinski   "Securing America's Interests in Iraq: The Remaining Options," *Military Technology*, March 2007.

Richard A. Clarke   "Admit It's Over," *New Republic*, November 27, 2006.

Ross Cohen   "Withdraw Decisively," *Washington Monthly*, June 2007.

Stephen F. Cohen   "Conscience and the War," *Nation*, March 26, 2007.

James Dobbins   "Who Lost Iraq?" *Foreign Affairs*, September-October 2007.

Robert Dreyfuss   "Apocalypse Not," *Washington Monthly*, March 2007.

Michael Duffy   "How to Leave Iraq," *Time*, July 19, 2007.

James D. Fearon   "Iraq's Civil War," *Foreign Affairs*, March-April 2007.

Peter W. Galbraith   "Divide Iraq," *New Republic*, November 27, 2006.

Leslie Gelb   "Would Defeat in Iraq Be So Bad?" *Time*, October 23, 2006.

Russell Warren Howe — "History vs. Statusquocracy: A Negotiated Partition in Iraq?" *Washington Report on Middle East Affairs*, July 2006.

Frederick W. Kagan — "Don't Abandon the Iraqis; The High Stakes of the War," *Weekly Standard*, May 28, 2007.

Peter Katel — "New Strategy in Iraq: Civil War?" *CQ Researcher*, February 23, 2007.

William Kristol and Frederick W. Kagan — "Congress Gives In on War Funding; Now Can We Fight the Enemy?" *Weekly Standard*, June 4, 2007.

Mother Jones — "Exiting Iraq: Now or Never?" November-December 2007.

David Nather — "Anti-war Movement Stuck in a Quaqmire," *CQ Weekly*, October 8, 2007.

Ned Parker — "Iraq Calmer, but More Divided," *Los Angeles Times*, December 10, 2007.

Charles Peters — "The Case for Facing Facts," *Newsweek*, December 3, 2007.

David Rieff — "Bring the Troops Home," *New Republic*, November 27, 2006.

Jonathan Schell — "Taking Power (Troop Withdrawal from Iraq)," *Nation*, October 8, 2007.

Stephen Schwartz — "Partition Iraq? No," *Weekly Standard*, June 19, 2007.

Anthony J.
Schwarz

"Iraq's Militias," *Parameters*, Spring
2007.

Matthew A.
Shadle and
Andrew J.
Bacevich

"No Exit from Iraq?" *Commonweal*,
October 12, 2007.

Garth Stewart

"Stay and Fight," *Washington
Monthly*, June 2007.

Stephen Zunes

"A Dangerous Division: The Senate's
Partition Plan for Iraq Will Make a
Tragic Situation Worse," *National
Catholic Reporter*, November 2, 2007.

Index

A

Abdul Aziz Al Saud, Abdullah bin (King), 36
Afghanistan
  al Qaeda, 56
  Bonn conference, 35
  non-combat power, 47
  redeployment, 59
  South Korean troops in, 22
  sustain fighting in, 51, 59
  Taliban, 39
  terrorists against, 19–20
  U.S. mess in, 44
  U.S. support of, 14
  voting in, 26
The Agency for International Development, 51
al Qaeda
  in Afghanistan, 56
  in Iran, 34
  in Iraq (AQI), 14, 33, 37, 74–76
  as jihadist threat, 82
  Pakistan against, 59
  reconstituted, 56
  recruiting tools, 37
  redeployment efforts, 59–60
  soft partition threat, 82
  Sunni insurgents, 27
  terrorism, 44, 56
  U.S. troops against, 27, 33, 64
  U.S. withdrawal, 27, 31, 56, 59–60
  violence, increasing, 12
  See also Terrorism/terrorists
Anbar Salvation Council, 75–76
Anti-jihadist battlefield, 39
Arab-Israeli conflict, 13

Articles of freedom, Iraq, 85–86
Asia
  democracy in, 17
  economic rebound, 19
  freedom, 25–26
  freedom in, 19, 25–26
  U.S. policy in, 20
Autonomous regions, Iraq, 83

B

Baghdad government, 40–41, 83
Bahrain, 59
Baker, James A., III, 11–16
Biddle, Stephen, 66–80
Biden, Joseph, 81–88
Bin Laden, Osama, 18, 24–25, 75
Biological weapons, 44
Bipartisanship, 42
Black Hawk Down incident, 31
Bonn conference, 35
Border security, Iraq, 72–74
Bosnia, 83
Bush, George H.W., 62–63
Bush, George W.
  Combat operations, 90–91
  government, Iraq, 9
  Iraq, as U.S. interest, 46–47
  Iraq policy, 30, 64, 92
  military withdrawal harmful, 8–9, 17–28
  national security team, 15
  staying the course, problems with, 54–55
  strategy, failure of, 56, 81
  surge policy, 9, 66–68
  two-state solution, 13–14
  U.S. troops in Iraq, 7, 33, 64